WATERFRONT TERMINALS AND OPERATIONS

Bernard Kempinski

KALMBACH BOOKS

WAUKESHA, WI

Dedication

I dedicate this book to the late Andy Sperandeo, the former editor of *Model Railroader*, who helped get me started in model railroad publishing, and to the late Frank Gustav, a merchant mariner who started sailing in convoys during World War II and was decorated for bravery in the Vietnam War, who kindled my interest in maritime subjects.

Kalmbach Books
21027 Crossroads Circle
Waukesha, Wisconsin 53186
www.KalmbachHobbyStore.com

Published in 2017
21 20 19 18 17   1 2 3 4 5

Manufactured in China

ISBN: 978-1-62700-265-3
EISBN: 978-1-62700-266-0

Editor: Randy Rehberg
Book Design: Tom Ford

Unless noted, photographs were taken by the author.

Library of Congress Control Number: 2016943711

Contents

1

CHAPTER ONE

Rail-marine operations

There is still plenty of fascinating railroad operation in North American harbors even if the nostalgic image of old-time steam railroading on the waterfront is long gone. In this scene, a triple consist of high-horsepower, 6-axle BNSF engines switches steel slab cars at the Pasha terminal in the Port of Los Angeles in 2014.

With a double blast of a steam whistle, the engineer slowly advances his train with a short cut of cars. Steel wheels squeal and clank as they bump onto the pontoon bridge that connects the tracks to the ancient wooden car float. The pontoon and the float tilt precariously from the sudden weight of the railcars, but the experienced engineer and his crew are unconcerned. They have done this hundreds of times before. They know the proper loading sequence, allowable tonnage, and switching procedures by heart. When the float is fully loaded, a colorfully painted steam tug bearing the logo of its railroad owner slips alongside. More steam whistle blasts announce their departure across the harbor.

Both steam and sailing ships are docked at South Street Seaport in New York City. The Brooklyn Bridge is visible in the distance.
Library of Congress

Scenes like this have captivated authors, journalists, filmmakers, and modelers for decades. Steam trains and tugs have long disappeared and been replaced by powerful diesel locomotives and tugs, long trains of specialized railcars, and ships so massive they are sometimes hard to fathom. Though most railroad car ferries are gone, rail-marine operations are still a vital aspect of modern transportation, **1**.

This book examines the railroad-marine interface—the terminal where railroad tracks meet the sea—from a model railroader's perspective. It focuses on the North American experience, but much of this information can apply to other parts of the world as well.

After a historic overview of rail-marine activity, I'll cover various major pier-side activities, such as break bulk or containers, or a commodity such as grain or minerals. These chapters include prototype information, photos of inspirational models, and a track

plan or two that demonstrate how each activity can be adapted to a model railroad. The book also contains a harbor project, a cargo project, a chapter on building ships—signature elements for rail-marine model railroads—and concludes with a look at modeling water and wharves.

Early rail-marine operations

From the earliest dugout canoes to the three-masted clipper ships of the 19th century, boats and ships were the fastest and most economical means of transportation. Although other modes of transportation have displaced them in terms of speed, ships remain the most cost efficient at moving freight long distances.

There is archaeological evidence that the Egyptians used rivers and canals for transportation as early as 4000 BC. Through the rise and fall of successive empires, the coastal inhabitants of the Mediterranean Basin and Pacific Ocean gradually

increased their ability to build ships and undertake more adventurous and dangerous voyages. The Phoenicians ventured as far as Britain. The Romans built a vast empire enriched by the maritime trade of wine, wheat, and gold. Chinese junks sailed much of the Pacific and Indian Oceans until 1500 AD, when the Confucian emperor curtailed trade by forbidding ships with more than two masts.

The importance of maritime transportation is evident when you look at the development of North America. The eastern American colonies and Canada all formed along coastal sites or up rivers. Several prominent early American cities—Albany, New York; Richmond, Virginia; and Washington, D.C.—are located at the furthest navigable points of their respective rivers. In 1860, New Orleans was the United States' busiest seaport.

For centuries, sailing ships represented the highest technology that civilizations could muster. Through

Workers unload a C&O canal boat along the Alexandria waterfront in this N scale diorama. A canal boat could carry 90–100 tons of coal, along with two mules and a crew. The rear cabin has living quarters for the crew, while the mules rested in the bow cabin.

the years of European exploration and colonization, the methods of cargo handling and stowage changed little; this did not change until the advent of the steam engine.

The 19th century industrial revolution changed everything. Populations increased and concentrated in cities where factories were located. Trade expanded to include manufactured goods, as well as food, for densely populated cities.

The steam engine was the heart of the industrial revolution. It powered stationary machines, ships, and a new mode of transportation—the railroad. Early steam engines were neither reliable nor efficient, so sailing ships managed to work in tandem with steamships during much of the 19th century, **2**. The advent of the compound steam engine made long-distance steamship voyages possible, relegating sailing ships to niche markets, such as the lumber trade and fishing, before they became totally obsolete.

Canals

Before the introduction of steam engines, canals, employing horse- or mule-drawn boats, played a part in developing North America beyond the coasts and rivers. While a horse could carry one-eighth of a ton, a canal barge pulled by a horse or two mules could carry almost 100 tons.

In the early 19th century, two canal systems emerged: one east of the Appalachians along the East Coast and one west of the Appalachians in the Midwest. (European countries also built extensive canal systems.)

The first North American canal system went from Montreal and along the St. Lawrence River to Lake Erie, with the completion of the Lachine Canal in 1825 and the Welland Canal in 1829, which bypassed Niagara Falls. The second was the Erie Canal system, completed in 1825, with a connection to Lake Ontario that was completed in 1828. Many smaller canals, such as the C&O Canal alongside the Potomac,

were built to carry coal from the Appalachians to East Coast cities, **3**.

In the Midwest, the canal system evolved to connect the Ohio River to Lake Erie, which enabled access to the western termini of the Erie and Welland Canals. The two most important Midwest canals were the Ohio & Erie Canal, completed in 1833, and the Wabash & Erie Canal, completed in 1853. A canal completed in 1848 between Chicago and the Illinois River helped Chicago become the most important transportation hub in North America.

North American canal development preceded development of the railroads by about 10 to 20 years. It is ironic that many of the first North American rail lines were developed to connect existing canals, which would eventually be totally supplanted by the railroads. For instance, in 1834, the Philadelphia & Columbia Railroad complemented the Schuylkill and Union Canals between Harrisburg

Crews load canal boats at the canal basin in Cumberland, Maryland, in the 19th century. They are using a mule to spot the iron pot hoppers on a trestle over a canal boat. The pot hoppers had doors that opened, which allowed the coal to fall into the waiting barge. *Library of Congress*

Jim Dalberg scratchbuilt these HO scale barges and a coal tipple based on the Port Delaware canal basin in Phillipsburg, New Jersey, on the Morris Canal. *Jim Dalberg*

and Philadelphia. The Allegheny Portage Railroad, the first railroad constructed through the Allegheny Mountains, linked two canal cities: Johnstown and Hollidaysburg. The first railroad in Canada, the Champlain & St. Lawrence, completed in 1838, connected the St. Lawrence River and Lake Champlain. These railway-to-canal connections incorporated some of the first rail-marine interfaces, and they provide some interesting modeling opportunities, **4** and **5**.

By the late 19th century, the great majority of canals were abandoned as they could not compete effectively with the spreading railway network. Canals that remain today are used for recreation except for the Welland Canal, which has been upgraded several times and is now part of the St. Lawrence Seaway, and the Illinois and Michigan Canal that linked Chicago to the Illinois River, which was supplemented by the Chicago Sanitary and Ship Canal in 1900.

Rivers

As canals lost importance, the United States began developing the Mississippi River system with locks and dams. Even before steamships made upstream voyages possible, the Mississippi and its tributaries were vital cargo arteries. President Lincoln, who called the Mississippi "the father of waters," had firsthand experience, as he made two trips as a young man floating cargo rafts down the Mississippi. Upon his arrival in New Orleans, he sold the cargo and raft, and then walked back to Illinois to do it again. The shallow-draft paddlewheel steamer made cargo transport on the Mississippi much more practical, **6**. Many early railroads

Locomotive no. 6 switches the wharf on Gerald McGee's layout set along the Mississippi River in 1906. A simple plank from the paddlewheel steamboat to the shore is all that is used to access the boat. *Todd McGee*

McCooks Landing was my freelanced layout that depicted a river port on the Tennessee River in 1864 during the American Civil War. Steamships and barges dock along the bank. The tracks parallel the bank between the river and a series of industries.

in the Midwest started by linking river ports to farm towns farther inland, **7**.

Now, the Mississippi is more than one big river. It is tied to a vast inland waterway system that stretches as far northwest as Montana and northeast to Pennsylvania. The inland waterway system is a key component of the nation's freight transportation network and includes about 12,000 miles of commercially navigable channels and

some 240 lock sites. In 2015, about 624 million tons of waterborne cargo transited the inland waterways, a volume that equaled about 14 percent of all intercity freight.

The map on page 9 depicts the geographic relationship of cargo tonnage for railroad lines and inland waterways in 2010, **8**. The heaviest railroad tonnage involved moving Powder River coal from Wyoming

southeast toward Kansas City. The BNSF line from Los Angeles to Kansas City also carried heavy tonnage, but that was mostly container traffic. However, the cargo artery with the greatest tonnage is the waterway traffic at the mouth of the Mississippi, **9**. The map illustrates the importance of New Orleans as a cargo transshipping terminus. It helps explain why such an important city is located there

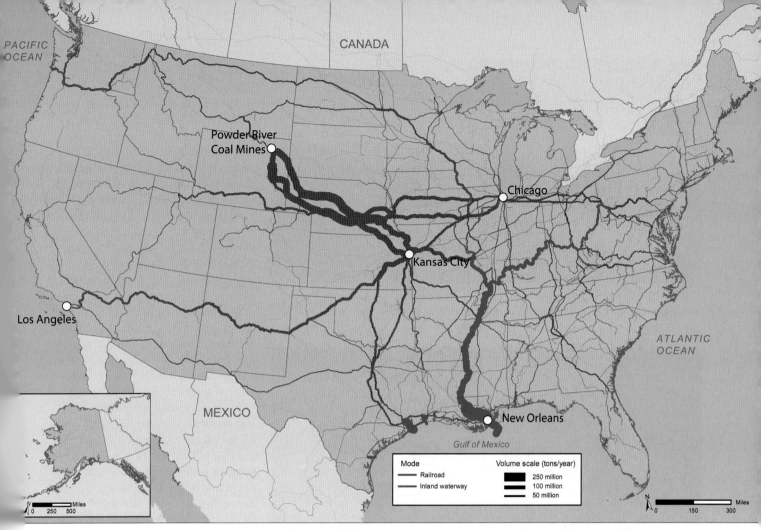

This map shows the geographical distribution of rail and freight arteries by cargo tonnage in the United States in 2010.
U.S. Department of Transportation

despite the ecological fragility of the area and its vulnerability to hurricanes. Now, New Orleans faces a man-made challenge. The expanded Panama Canal, completed in 2016, allows ships with up to a 50-foot draft to traverse it, but the lower Mississippi stretch carrying ocean vessels to the ports of New Orleans, Baton Rouge, and south Louisiana is currently only 45 feet deep. Deeper dredging would be extremely costly.

It is difficult to appreciate the carrying capacity of a contemporary barge until you understand how much tonnage a single barge can move. A standard dry cargo barge can move as much cargo as 70 trucks or 16 railcars. Fifteen barges pushed or pulled by a single tug is a common tow configuration on America's inland rivers, although lash-ups can vary from 1 to 30 barges, **10**. A typical 15-barge tow can haul as much dry cargo as two unit trains or 1,050 trucks while using

less fuel and creating fewer emissions. (Chapter 6 has more information about tugs and barges.)

The possibilities for riverine-based rail-marine modeling and operations, even in areas far from the coast, should not be overlooked.

Great Lakes

The Great Lakes also played a key role in development of North American transportation. Early explorers traveled the Great Lakes in search of fur, and the lakes played an important role in the War of 1812. But it wasn't until the 1840s when the Great Lakes became busy with commercial cargo traffic such as wheat, corn, lumber, coal, and iron ore. Lumber from the region's vast pine forests made Chicago the world's busiest lumber port during the 1870s.

Crops from Midwestern farms crossed the lakes to markets in the East. From 1831 to 1888, wheat was the primary bulk cargo carried on the

Great Lakes. By the 1930s, it was still the leading grain carried on the lakes. (See chapter 3 for the rail-marine aspects of grain shipment.)

Iron ore from the region traveled east on ships that returned filled with coal from Pennsylvania. Iron mines in Michigan's Marquette Range supplied all the iron ore shipped on the Great Lakes until 1877. The first ore dock was built at Marquette, Michigan, in 1857. It was flat rather than elevated, and the vessels were loaded by wheelbarrow. Later designs took advantage of gravity to unload railroad cars and fill the holds of waiting ships. Iron ore is now the leading commodity by tonnage on the Great Lakes. (Chapter 4 contains information on iron and other mineral rail-marine terminals.)

Canals helped the Great Lakes prosper. The state of Michigan built St. Marys Falls Ship Canal, called the Soo Locks, from 1853 to 1855, and

The lower Mississippi River is the busiest freight artery in the United States. Here, barge and ship traffic transports export cargo on the Mississippi River in the Port of New Orleans on September 9, 2005. *Bob Nichols, U.S. Department of Agriculture*

A 12-barge tow enters Pickwick Lock in Counce, Tennessee, October 24, 2013. Pickwick is one of nine Tennessee Valley Authority navigation locks on the Tennessee River, which is part of the Mississippi River waterway system. *Fred Tucker, U.S. Army Corps of Engineers*

The 1,000-foot-long, self-unloading bulk carrier *American Century* passes the Edison Sault hydroelectric power plant on St. Marys River below the Soo Locks, Sault Ste. Marie, Michigan. Ships this size cannot leave the upper Great Lakes as they are too big for the Welland Canal. *Richard McDonald, U.S. Army Corps of Engineers*

opened Lake Superior to markets and industries along the lower lakes.

The completion of the St. Lawrence Seaway in 1959 opened the Great Lakes to oceangoing maritime traffic. The seaway connected Montreal, an ocean port, and the Great Lakes through a series of locks and canals including the Welland Canal.

Today, shippers use the St. Lawrence Seaway and the Great Lakes system to primarily move bulk cargo, such as grain, iron ore, coal, and petroleum products, which comprises 90 percent of the traffic. General cargo such as containers, steel, and machinery accounts for the remaining 10 percent. This freight allocation is due to relative speed. Railways can ship general cargo and containers faster to eastern and western seaboard ports than it can go through the seaway. For example, a high-priority container shipment by rail from Chicago to Montreal takes about one day, while it would take around one week on a ship via the Great Lakes and the seaway. Conversely, bulk cargoes are not as time sensitive. Additionally, the fact that the seaway is closed for about three months over winter does not meet the demands of current "just-in-time" supply chain logistics.

The seaway can accommodate ships up to 766 feet long and 80 feet wide with about 25,000-ton displacement. This ship class is also referred to as *Seawaymax* since it is designed to fit specifically in the seaway's locks. This is relatively small compared to current oceangoing ships, called *salties*, that can be over 1,000 feet long. The Soo Locks can handle lake boats up to 1,000 feet long, but those boats are confined to the upper lakes of Superior, Michigan, Huron, and Erie, **11**. (Vessels on the Great Lakes are called boats regardless of their size.) They cannot venture east past the Welland Canal.

Oceans

By virtue of its geography with oceans on east, west, and southern coasts, the United States is a maritime nation. The role of maritime commerce in the United States cannot be overstated. Even before the nation's founding, the

Locomotive no. 1, a 4-4-0 On30 engine, brings the morning passenger train onto Cranberry Wharf in time to meet the ferry. The scene is on Troels Kirk's Coast Line Railroad. The freelanced layout is set in Maine during the 1920s. *Troels Kirk*

Dick Patterson built a beautifully scenicked HOn30 layout based on the Dolly Varden Railway. The model structure here is based on the Dolly Varden Mine Railway ore bunker situated on the Alice Arm, a fiord-like extension of the Pacific Ocean. *Dave Frary*

American colonies were famous for their ships and sailors. Prior to the American Civil War, almost all federal revenue came from customs and duties collected on foreign trade.

After World War II, the United States, with its large fleet of war surplus freighters, fed by railroad marine terminals, dominated world trade. Most of it was transatlantic in nature. That started to change between 1960 and 1990, when the worldwide share of transatlantic traffic showed a relative decline as Asian maritime trade expanded. During the past decade, many rising United States trade partners in Asia surpassed their European counterparts and are challenging, or even exceeding, U.S. trade partners in North America (in terms of merchandise trade value). China became the second largest U.S. trading partner in 2006, surpassing Mexico. China also appears to be on

Cundy's Harbor is the terminus of a short branch on Bob Hayden's previous Carrabasset & Dead River HOn30 layout. *Dave Frary*

Dave Frary and Hal Reynolds built this On30 scale scene as part of a display for the Nantucket Whaling Museum. The layout depicts the Nantucket Central Railroad Company, a three-foot narrow gauge railroad on the island of Nantucket. That railroad linked the villages of Nantucket and Siasconset. *Hal Reynolds*

track to top Canada's total trade value with the United States. Container vessels carry the majority of China's trade value, whereas container trade accounts for only a fraction of the value of U.S.-Canada trade.

In 2010, the United States imported about 12 percent of world merchandise trade and exported about 8 percent, according to the World Trade Organization. Ships carried a large

portion of this. The U.S. Department of Transportation reported that in 2010 ocean vessels carried 53 percent of U.S. imports and 38 percent of exports by value, the largest share of any mode, although land exports accounted for 33 percent. More than 62,000 vessels—about 172 a day—called at U.S. seaports in 2010. Tankers and container ships accounted for about two-thirds of the vessel calls.

The widespread adoption of containerization has had a major effect on the nature of world trade. Prior to containerization, loading or unloading a ship was a very expensive and time-consuming task, and a cargo ship typically spent more time docked than at sea. (Chapter 7 has more about container shipping.)

In addition to foreign trade, North American ports used to conduct considerable maritime trade with each other. This is called *short sea, coastwise,* or *intracoastal shipping.* For much of the 19th and 20th centuries, North American ports shipped coal, lumber, grain, and general cargo to each other. Now, North American short sea shipping competes with railroads for long distances, and trucking for short distances. With present railroads and trucks being so efficient, short sea shipping now only serves niche markets and provides feeder service to the East and to Gulf Coast ports from Caribbean transshipment hubs such as Kingston, Freeport, Cartagena, and Panama.

Narrow gauge railroad waterfronts

Narrow gauge railroads and their waterfront terminals present an interesting and colorful footnote to the rail-marine model railroad genre. Many model railroaders think of spindly trestles spanning mountain chasms when narrow gauge railroads are mentioned. They may not be aware of the extensive use of narrow gauge railroads to link harbors with land-side industries. Narrow gauge railroads terminated at harbors in many of North America's coastal regions. Perhaps the best known were the harbors that served the Maine two-foot railroads such as the Wiscasset, Waterville & Farmington harbor at its namesake city, Wiscasset. Modelers have been inspired to create waterfront layouts featuring Maine two-footers in a variety of gauges including the correct-to-scale HOn2 and On2 as well as the more popular HOn30 and On30, **12, 14,** and **16.**

Aside from Maine, there were many other locations where narrow gauge railroads maintained waterfront terminals including Alaska, California, Louisiana, Hawaii, Massachusetts, and Virginia in the United States, and Yukon and British Columbia in Canada.

One of the more interesting was the Dolly Varden Mine Railway on the coast of Alice Arm, British Columbia, **13.** This pint-sized railroad served a small but rich silver mine. The 18-mile-

16

Forney engine no. 2 shifts a flatcar on the deck of Cranberry Wharf on Troels Kirk's On30 narrow gauge model railroad. *Troels Kirk*

long route passed through spectacular coastal mountain scenery.

The White Pass and Yukon Railway was a three-foot gauge railway that still has some portions active in tourist service. In its prime years, it had waterfronts at both ends: Skagway on the Pacific and Whitehorse on the Yukon River.

Nantucket had a tiny three-foot gauge railroad, the Nantucket Central Railroad Company, that primarily served tourists to the island, **15.**

Louisiana once had an extensive array of narrow gauge railroads that served sugar plantations. The first

was probably built in 1833 on Little Versailles Plantation in St. James Parish. At its peak in 1925, southern Louisiana had more than 150 plantation railroads, 3,000 miles of track, 500 locomotives, and more than 15,000 pieces of rolling stock.

Hauling cane was the chief business, but they also had other uses. A spur usually went down to the bayou from the mill to haul processed sugar and molasses to the landing, where a steamboat would pick them up. Supplies brought to the plantation by the steamboat were also hauled from the water's edge aboard the trains.

1

CHAPTER TWO

Break bulk piers and terminals

A classic example of the labor-intensive break bulk process. Longshoremen unload bananas from a steamship to an FGE reefer in New Orleans in the early 20th century. *Library of Congress*

Before World War II, most maritime cargo transport was in the form of general cargo or *break bulk*. The term originates from the nautical phrase "to break bulk," which means "begin to unload cargo." Shipping vessels often had a mix of cargo on board, with loose materials, liquids, and general cargo all in the same vessel. It was a tedious process of manually loading and unloading, packing, and repacking. The task was never easy when involving barrels, sacks, crates, and dunnage.

A steamer lays alongside a break bulk pier shed in this model-genic scene at Southern Railway Terminals in Mobile, Alabama. In the background, there is a coaling station with chutes for loading ships and an inclined ramp for coal hoppers. *Library of Congress*

High risk of accidents, loss of cargo, and theft made the process risky for the worker and for the shipper. Shippers developed specialized lifting equipment, sacks designated for coffee beans, and pallets for goods, which helped improve efficiency slightly, but it was still a labor-intensive task.

The longshoremen who moved the cargo bundled it together as pieces or units that they could manipulate—the so-called "man load." Examples include bags of sugar, cotton bales, drums of liquids, and bunches of bananas, **1**. The workers carried loads of 50 to 100 pounds on their backs in and out of vessels, into sheds, and on and off trucks and railcars. It was not uncommon for a package to be handled

between 30 and 50 times before reaching its final destination.

Break bulk required a lot of manual labor when there was a ship to work. If there was no ship, there was no work and no pay. Longshoremen would arrive at the docks in the morning seeking employment for the day. The gang boss would select the work crews, using whatever criteria suited his fancy. This process was essentially the same across the world. In the United States, it was called *shaping*.

The process was rife with corruption, as immortalized in the movie *On the Waterfront*. Workers often had to provide kickbacks to gang bosses to get an assignment. In the United States, the labor

situation slowly became less chaotic through unionization and government regulations.

The labor-intensive break bulk process was also slow, and ships had to spend a lot of time in port. Ship turnaround times were long, which resulted in ships remaining in port sometimes exceeding the time they spent at sea. Long port times hurt efficiency. A ship that stands still does not make money. As unlikely as it seems, it took until the 20th century for things to change.

Design of pier sheds

The break bulk handling process and the related infrastructure at any given pier reflected the particular conditions

3

Mat Thompson modeled a break bulk pier and shed on his HO scale Oregon Coast Railway. The shed is a Walthers kit while the ship is from Sylvan Models. *Paul Dolkos*

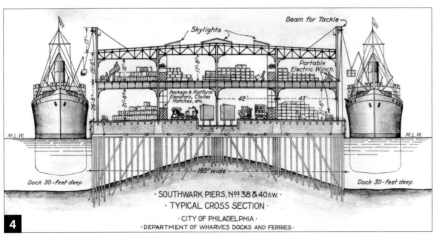

4

This cross section shows typical construction and activity at a pier in the first half of the 20th century. Note the tracks in the middle of the shed and the cargo being moved using tackle attached to the cargo masts on the shed. *Library of Congress*

of that harbor. It also changed over time as conditions changed.

Break bulk could be delivered straight from a truck or train onto a ship, but it was more common for the cargo to be delivered to the dock in advance of a ship's arrival with the cargo stored in warehouses. When the ship arrived, longshoremen carried the cargo from the warehouse to the pier to be loaded on the ship. Due to the time-consuming nature of break bulk operations, workers had to unload, sort, and repack the cargo on the dock. This led to the development in the later 19th century of having sheds on piers.

Cargo could be moved directly to railroad cars on the pier as an alternative to storing it on the pier or in the warehouse for later removal. Some design engineers favored tracks on the outside margin of the pier to allow cargo to be deposited directly into the car from the ship, **2**. The tracks were set flush in the pavement so that wagons and trucks could also use the margin.

However, when a cargo was not yet sorted, or when the right railroad car was not on the pier promptly as the cargo was being unloaded, the trains occupying prime work space could interfere with the unloading. Experience showed that railroad cars were typically slower to load and unload than a ship. Consequently, this system could cause backups on the busy pier margin. Placing tracks down the center of piers offered the advantage of keeping the pier margin clear, **3** and **4**. Both designs were common, and you should consult your prototype to decide what type you should include on your layout. If you have a choice, tracks on the margin would provide easier access for switching and uncoupling on a model railroad.

Pier sheds were initially made from wood, but wood was vulnerable to rot and fire. Thus, steel and concrete quickly replaced wood in new construction when they became available.

Some pier sheds had two or more stories, so longshoremen had to move cargo between the levels of the pier, as well as move cargo on and off ships. To accomplish such interior transfers, pier sheds had elevators for packages, larger elevators for trucks, and cargo chutes (slides) for sending bags or bales of cargo from the upper story to the lower.

Facades of the head houses on pier sheds often featured elaborate architecture with arches and decorative trim that reflected the area's character, **5**.

Cranes and mechanical hoists

Apart from the ancient tread-wheel cranes powered by humans walking like hamsters inside a circular wheel, longshoremen generally used a ship's own masts and gear to sling-load break bulk that was too big to carry by hand on planks, **6**.

By the 20th century, the general practice along the Atlantic Coast, and in some places on the Pacific Coast, was to use cargo masts built on the top of pier sheds. These were structural steel or wooden frames high above a shed's roof to which pulleys or blocks could be attached practically at any point alongside a pier, **7**. This was an exceedingly simple and effective method of handling freight, although it took time to set up. Later piers had gantry cranes spanning the aprons. These cranes could move up and down the pier as needed. Ship's gear could also be used if land-based cranes were not available at the pier.

To avoid crowded waterfront facilities, some ships unloaded their cargoes into railroad cars carried on barges. These barges then carried the railroad cars to a rail yard located away from the central waterfront for assembly into trains. Cargo was also transferred from ships onto covered barges called *lighters*, **8**. Specialized cargo-handling equipment, such as grain elevators, was also mounted on barges and taken out to the ships.

After World War II, shippers began to build dedicated merchant vessels designed for specific kinds of cargo such as bales of wool, logs, and liquid bulk. Those ships created economies of scale by handling cargoes of just one type, and they gained importance. But the bottleneck on the dock side kept major advancements at bay. The introduction of shipping containers in the 1950s revolutionized the shipping industry and changed the nature of traditional break bulk.

Pier 16 in San Francisco incorporates a southwest style architecture with a stucco finish typical of California. *Library of Congress*

Longshoremen use the ship's gear and rigging to load lumber from a flatcar to a steamer in Gulfport, Mississippi. *Library of Congress*

On Pier 1 in Baltimore, you can see cargo masts on a pier shed. Longshoremen used the steel frames to secure blocks and tackle to move break bulk. In this 2015 photo, the restored Liberty Ship *John W. Brown* stands in contrast to the weathered pier shed.

This remarkable photo is a panorama created using two images of the Holland America Line Terminal in Hoboken, New Jersey, in 1904. It illustrates the diversity of rail-marine activity and infrastructure discussed in this chapter. *Library of Congress*

Used BN engines are heading to export customers at the Port of Houston. The foreground shows a wide diversity of break bulk cargo that the port handles. *Dick Knoll*

Contemporary break bulk

Containerization did not eliminate the shipping of break bulk. Instead, it changed in nature from loose cargo to specialization of handling goods that are too challenging to transport in containers or where containerization does not represent a valid or cost-efficient proposition.

The modern definition of break bulk is general cargo, loaded as individual or bundled pieces, not stowed into a container, nor transported in ship-sized liquid or dry bulk loads. Break bulk cargo can be as big as a 200-ton industrial boiler that occupies the entire deck of a heavy-lift ship to cargo on pallets which, due to specific cargo-related attributes, cannot be transported in containers, such as large sacks of rice. Shipping specialists list no less than 150 break bulk cargo types divided into a number of larger categories. Some of these include project cargo, steel products, forest products, bags, bales, and perishable food.

Project cargo is the transportation of large, heavy, high value, or critical (to the project they are intended for) pieces of equipment. Also commonly referred to as *heavy lift*, this includes shipments made of various components that need disassembly for shipment and reassembly after delivery. Examples include power generation equipment (generators, turbines, wind turbines), equipment for the oil and gas industry, subsea systems, cables on reels, gas tanks, modules, petrochemical plant equipment, mining equipment, building and construction equipment, brewery tanks, silos, and heavy machinery such as locomotives or railcars, **9** and **10**. Large windmill parts are a common project cargo that sometimes goes from ship to rail (see chapter 9).

Moving large project cargo can be a complex operation involving logistics experts to coordinate specialized vehicles, structural engineers to make sure loading and stowing is done safely and securely, and government officials to coordinate road clearance and security.

Iron and steel products such as coils, plates, steel bars, slabs, plates, steel wire, pipes, and tubes are dense items that frequently move in unit loads by break bulk ships.

Forest products include all kinds of wood and paper products. Whole logs are a common unit cargo on ships from the northwest Pacific Coast of North America.

Bags with loose cargo such as malt, fertilizer, sugar, and rice and baled goods such as cotton sometimes can be moved more efficiently without being placed in containers.

Perishable cargo that requires refrigeration but is not containerized is also considered break bulk, **11**. The reefer ships in this trade have interiors that resemble refrigerated warehouses. They usually can also take refrigerated containers on deck.

Contemporary break bulk terminals still use pier sheds, but cargo mast hoists have become obsolete. For several decades, rail-mounted gantry cranes were common, **12**. Lately, the trend in pier-side cranes is toward wheel-mounted mobile harbor cranes, **13** and **14**. HO scale modelers are in luck as die-cast models of Gottwald and Liebherr mobile cranes are available in this scale.

Port of Davisville

A modern break bulk port can make for a manageable model railroad. The track plan on page 21 depicts the Port of Davisville near Kingstown, Rhode Island. Located near the mouth of Narragansett Bay, the Port of Davisville is part of Quonset Terminals, the largest transshipment facility in the region. The port offers four berths and five terminals with 58 acres of terminal storage.

The Seaview Transportation Company provides railroad service to the port using a handful of locomotives running over 14 miles of track that wrap around the former Quonset Naval Air Station. (The navy base closed in the 1970s.) Seaview Transportation's rail operations connect to Class 1 carriers via the Providence & Worcester Railroad. On-dock rail allows them to transfer cargo directly from ship or barge to railcar.

In addition to the port, Seaview Transportation's railroad handles other business of the Quonset Terminals

10 Ship cranes load a 150-ton transformer directly to a depressed center railcar. *Port of Palm Beach*

11 Two refrigerated boxcars at frozen food processor Seafreeze, Ltd. await pickup by Seaview locomotive no. 5, a venerable SW-7. *Nathan Lafond*

Rail-mounted gantry cranes work at Locust Point, Baltimore. This type of crane is still in use, but they are becoming less common.

Mobile harbor cranes, like the Liebherr 500 shown here at Rukert Terminals in Baltimore, are becoming common in North American waterfronts. Die-cast HO scale models of this crane are available.

including frozen food, automobile shipping, plastic products, and lumber. There are extensive transloading areas throughout Quonset Terminals to handle large shipments.

Seaview handled more than 5,000 carloads in a recent year, including products shipped from local area industries, products that arrived for distribution throughout New England, and shipments that arrived at the Port of Davisville.

Another major customer is North Atlantic Distribution (NORAD), a privately owned company located at the port. NORAD is one of the largest auto importers in North America, serving as a port of entry, processing center, and distribution hub for imported and domestic vehicles including some luxury brands such as Bentley and Porsche. The railroad ships these cars on auto racks to customers in the region and throughout the United States.

The railroad also provides service to Seafreeze, Ltd., the largest producer of frozen fish on the East Coast, which supplies frozen fish to a world-wide range of markets, including bait products to domestic and international longline fleets.

The track plan is 12 by 18 feet and could fit in a garage or basement rec room. Access to the layout is from the right-hand side. The plan loosely follows the prototype track arrangement as there was not sufficient room to show all the elements of this interesting railroad. The Seaview interchanges with the Providence & Worcester main line at the lower right. Amtrak and the MBTA also use that line. Two industries are situated off the left side of the interchange yard. The Seaview line wraps around the corner to a junction of the two main branches. One heads to the port, while the second heads to the central peninsula. Toray Plastics is a major customer, although Senesco Marine and General Dynamics Electric Boat Division do not get direct rail service.

The port has several tracks that require service including an auto rack yard and the Seafreeze factory. Wind turbines have been a common cargo handled by the port in recent years.

Seaview Transportation's GP-10 locomotive waits to haul two depressed center flatcars with transformer loads. In the background, a Gottwald 7680 mobile harbor crane with a 150-ton capacity has just finished lifting the transformers from the barge. *Nathan Lafond*

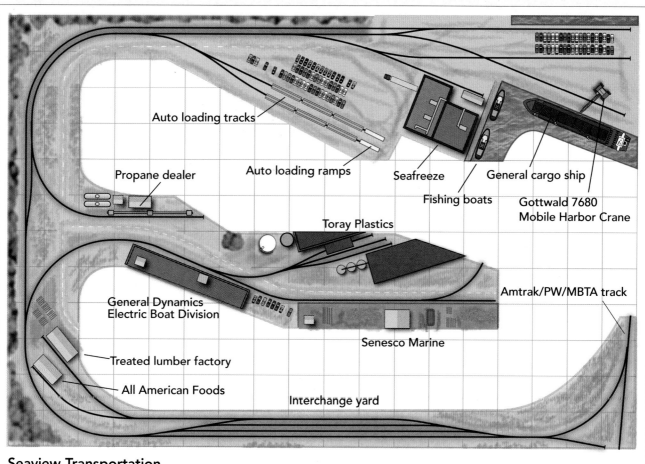

Auto loading tracks

Propane dealer

Auto loading ramps

Seafreeze

General cargo ship

Fishing boats

Gottwald 7680
Mobile Harbor Crane

Toray Plastics

General Dynamics
Electric Boat Division

Senesco Marine

Amtrak/PW/MBTA track

Treated lumber factory

All American Foods

Interchange yard

Seaview Transportation

Scale: HO
Size: 12 x 18 feet
Prototype: Port of Davisville

Era: 2016
Style: Shelf
Mainline run: 60 feet

Minimum radius: 30"
Turnouts: No. 6
Train length: 10–12 cars

Scale of plan:
⅜" = 1 foot, 12" grid

1

CHAPTER THREE

Grain terminals

Marine grain elevators are large complex structures that could be the focus of a model railroad. This is Bunge's grain elevator on the Mississippi River in Destrehan, Louisiana, part of the Port of New Orleans. *U.S. Department of Agriculture*

The grain trade is nearly as old as grain growing. In the ancient world, outlying farms shipped grain to the centers of great empires. Early granaries were simple earthen jugs, but over the years, the technology evolved.

When Europeans settled North America, it became one of the world's great breadbaskets. Through the 19th century, agricultural products comprised about three-quarters of all U.S. exports, with grain being the biggest component, especially later in the century.

In the 21st century, the United States is still a major supplier of grain to the world. The United States produces only 10 percent of world's wheat, but it is consistently the world's biggest wheat exporter. The United States accounts for about 2 percent of the world's rice production, but it ships about 10 percent of the world's rice exports. The United States is the world's largest soybean producer and second largest soybean exporter, contributing 34 percent of the world's soybean production and 33 percent of world's soybean exports. Finally, the United States is the world's largest producer and exporter of corn, although 85 percent of U.S. production is used domestically. Canada is also a major grain exporter and ranks in the top seven of the world's wheat producers and exporters.

The grain transport system uses trucks, trains, barges, and ships to move the grain and grain elevators to store it. The patterns of transportation for moving this grain has changed over the years, but there usually was a grain elevator at each point where the grain changed transportation modes, especially at the water's edge, **1**. Such a waterfront grain terminal can be the centerpiece of a layout.

In the 19th century, grain in the United States moved primarily eastward across the country from the Midwest to the Northeast by way of Buffalo, New York, and the Erie Canal. Civil engineering projects launched during the Great Depression helped open a new north-to-south route by improving transportation on the Mississippi River and its tributaries. At the end of World War II, grain exports grew significantly as U.S. farm productivity increased and the Midwest became a global source of grain. By the 1950s, shipments of grain were moving all the way down the Mississippi River to the Gulf of Mexico.

In 1855, investors built the steam-powered Pioneer Mills on the waterfront in Alexandria, Virginia. It could receive grain directly from ships using a marine leg. Railcars could also deliver sacks of grain via a team track one block away. This scene is in a diorama I built for the Lyceum, Alexandria's History Museum.

Workers at Union Grain elevator in Toledo, Ohio, use a marine leg to unload a four-masted sailing ship. A steam locomotive is visible at the far left. *Library of Congress*

Early grain transportation

Prior to 1827, getting surplus grain that grew abundantly in the Midwest to eastern markets required transportation over long and difficult routes. Some growers sent grain from the Midwest on flatboats down the Ohio and Mississippi Rivers to New Orleans, where it was loaded onto sailing vessels that carried it to its eventual destinations in the East or in Europe. Others sent it by wagon on rough roads that passed over the rugged Appalachian Mountains. Neither option was easy or inexpensive. More often than not, when the grain reached its destination, it had spoiled and was unusable.

When the Erie Canal opened in 1825, it became the first efficient transportation system to breach the Appalachians. Since Buffalo was situated on the western end of the Erie Canal and the eastern end of the Great Lakes, it became an important transshipping hub. Midwestern grain could be shipped by lake boats to Buffalo, where the Erie Canal would take the grain to New York City.

Thanks to the canal, freight charges dropped from $100 to $10 a ton for grain shipments. But the process was still cumbersome as laborers had to manually move the grain from ships to canal boats since even the smallest lake boats were

Grain elevators and marine legs were invented and used extensively in Buffalo, New York. Buffalo was an important grain transshipment point during much of the 19th century. *Library of Congress*

Grain scoopers in the hold of a ship help move the last bit of grain toward a marine leg. *Library of Congress*

too large for use on the Erie Canal and canal boats were too small for lake travel. Handling the grain by hand was slow and arduous work that caused delays.

The grain transloading problem became more manageable in 1842, when Joseph Dart, a Buffalo grain merchant, built the world's first grain elevator along the Buffalo River. Dart came up with the idea of unloading grain ships by means of an endless belt of buckets, a system already used inside mills for moving grain and flour.

Dart's elevator consisted of a grain warehouse, a wooden structure with storage bins for the grain. Attached to this was a "marine leg." Inside the marine leg was a steam-driven belt with buckets attached to it. The marine leg could move slightly up and down. When operators lowered the leg into a ship's hold, it could reach the pile of grain. As the belt turned, the buckets would take a bite out of the grain in the hold and carry it to bin on the top of the structure (the *garner*). There, scales attached to the garner weighed the grain. By means of gravity, various chutes and tubes allowed the grain to be sorted and distributed to any number of tall grain bins within the granary. (The term *elevator* originated because the process elevated the grain from the ship and stored it in bins until it was lowered for transshipment or milling purposes.)

The first elevator was small but highly successful, and later versions were even more capable, **2–4**. One improvement featured a second elevator that would lift the grain from the garner to the top of bins taller than the marine leg. These improved elevators could unload a ship at the rate of more than 1,000 bushels per hour. It soon became common practice to have a ship arrive at port, unload, and leave the very same day. This was unheard of before Dart's elevator.

Grain merchants discovered that grain elevators also made ideal storage facilities for grain. In each of an elevator's bins, the grain was kept dry, cool, and free from pests such as rats, birds, and worms that could wipe out the entire load. It was also possible to

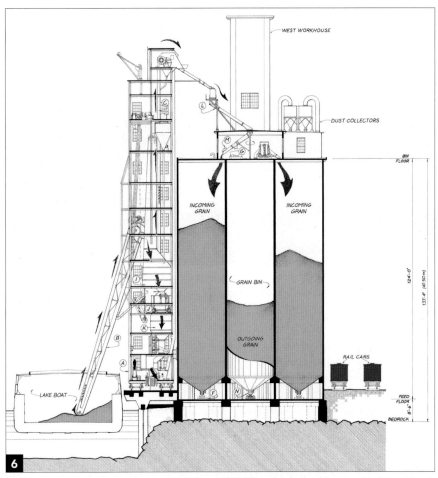

This drawing illustrates how a typical grain elevator and marine leg worked to unload a ship. The marine tower here is movable. *Library of Congress*

Three large grain elevators dominated the waterfront on Doug Tagsold's Toledo Terminal layout.

I built this N scale grain elevator based on the former PRR and Central Soya terminal in Canton, Maryland, in the Port of Baltimore.

The Archer Daniels Midland grain elevator in Ama, Louisiana, utilizes a loop track to simplify unloading of unit grain trains. Loop and balloon tracks are common at North American grain terminals. *U.S. Department of Agriculture*

This is Portland's Louis Dreyfus grain elevator from the west bank of the Willamette River. Building the intricate elevators, conveyors, and loading spouts would be a fun and challenging project.

weigh the grain as it was being stored and take samples of the grain to check for purity and contaminants.

Other grain merchants built grain elevators in and around Buffalo Harbor, having a capacity to store more than 1.5 million bushels of grain. In a short time, Buffalo became the world's largest grain port. Similar grain elevators then sprouted up all over the United States and around the world. Typically, grain elevators were found at both ends of the journey when grain moved by ship.

In 1864, the steam power shovel was patented, a device that directed grain to the marine leg buckets. The shovel was a large metal scoop operating off the grain elevator's power supply through a complicated system of ropes that was rigged in the hold of a ship and operated by men who became known as *grain scoopers*, **5**. Scoopers sometimes had to shovel and sweep the last of the grain in the hold into the buckets to get it all. The elevator and power shovel contributed greatly to reducing the cost of shipping wheat from the farms in the Midwest to Eastern markets.

Marine towers, in which the marine leg is housed, could either be in a fixed position or movable on car wheels, **6**. With a fixed tower, a boat's crew had to move the lake boat so the marine leg could get all the grain from the holds. A movable tower could reach a number of holds, but not all of them, so some ship movements were still required. Power shovels could drag the length of a boat's hold in order to bring grain within reach of the marine leg. As early as 1905, some marine legs used the pneumatic principle, a system of air flowing through a tube to suck up grain like a giant vacuum sweeper, but bucket legs still remained in use.

Although the grain elevator was invented in Buffalo, grain elevators became the heart of the transportation system that developed in Chicago. In the middle of the 19th century, Chicago was becoming an important rail hub for livestock, lumber, and grain. Shippers started diverting grain from ships to trains because trains were faster and more direct. As the railroads expanded like a spider's web into the surrounding country, farmers were able to get their crops placed in sacks and delivered from the prairies to the marketplace more quickly. As business increased, more and more sacks of grain piled up in Chicago.

Eventually, the simple, but inefficient, sack had to go. In 1857, the Chicago Board of Trade introduced a wheat grading system, so one farmer's crop could be combined and stored in bulk with another farmer's crop of the same grade. The loose grain could be loaded in boxcars equipped with grain doors and then mechanically transferred from railroad cars to grain elevators, which eliminated the need for laborers to load and unload sacks. The seller would walk off with a warehouse receipt, which he could trade, sell, or use as currency in the marketplace. From the grain elevator, a buyer could have his grain transferred directly into a boat to be carried anywhere around the globe.

Grain elevators began popping up all across the prairies. By 1861, Chicago's grain trade had increased to 50 million bushels annually—an increase of more than 48 million bushels in a decade. The grading system also led to the idea of trading grain futures, a financial business that is still headquartered in Chicago.

Marine terminal grain elevators can also receive grain directly from railcars. In the days when boxcars carried grain, terminal designers employed various systems to unload the cars. At first, men used axes to cut the grain doors, and shovels and brooms to unload the cars. Around 1920, tilting boxcar unloaders came into use. The tilting unloaders grabbed the whole boxcar, lifted it, and then tilted it. The car first tilted sideways to an 30-degree angle, while at the same time a mechanical door opener pressed against the grain door which is pushed inside the car as it tilted. To accelerate the flow, the car, still inclined at a 30-degree angle, was tipped endways to a 45-degree angle. The tilter then tipped endways in the other direction, so the grain rushed out first from one end and then from the other. When the grain ran out, crews used an air hose to clean the residual amount while the car was brought back

A Union Pacific mixed freight rounds the curve on the mainline tracks alongside the Louis Dreyfus grain elevator in Portland, Oregon.

Bulk carrier *Sophie Oldendorff* uses a self-unloader to transfer aggregate at Carroll Street Wharf near Harbor Island, Beaumont, Texas. *Port of Beaumont*

to its original position. The clamps then released the car. The whole operation of unloading a car in this manner took about 7–10 minutes. This system also allowed the grain doors to be recycled, which resulted in cost savings.

Boxcar unloaders became obsolete when railroads switched to covered hoppers to carry grain. Covered hoppers unload through the doors on the bottoms of the hoppers, a much simpler and faster unloading process.

Railroads take over

Buffalo's role in transshipment of grain decreased, while Chicago's increased, once railroads proved faster and more

reliable than using lake boats and canal boats. Buffalo reached its peak as a grain center in the 1920s and again during World War II. However, since that time, the decline in Buffalo's grain transshipping was steady and severe. In 1932, the Welland Canal opened, and this spelled the beginning of the end for the Buffalo grain industry. The canal was able to accommodate full-sized grain boats coming from the upper Great Lakes ports, bypassing Buffalo, as these boats delivered their cargo to Lake Ontario ports for transshipment. The final blow came in 1959 with the opening of the St. Lawrence Seaway. This waterway gave moderate size

Beaumont stevedores unload an Army MRAP vehicle from the hold of a break bulk ship. *U.S. Army*

ocean vessels passage into the interior of North America through the Great Lakes, completely cutting Buffalo out of the shipping chain.

Other cities on the Great Lakes developed major marine grain terminals including Toledo, Duluth, and Milwaukee, **7**. In Duluth, ore docks rivaled grain elevators in terms of physical scale, but the grain elevators had greater economic impact than the famous ore piers. Duluth's first steam-powered grain elevator was constructed in 1869. It held 350,000 bushels—just 20 percent the capacity of its modern counterparts. Since then, dozens of grain elevators were built, destroyed, or abandoned on the city's waterfront, enhanced by the construction of a ship canal across the narrow spit of Minnesota Point. One of the more famous grain companies was the Peavey Company, which built the first circular concrete grain silo in 1900. Several grain elevators are still in operation, and in 2010, they shipped more than 2.7 million tons of grain.

During much of the 20th century, ports along the East Coast had grain elevators that were rail served. Just about every major railroad owned a grain elevator situated for ocean shipping. Some were quite large, like the former PRR elevator in Canton, Maryland, **8**. But in the 21st century, most of these grain elevators closed. Their older designs

could not compete with the newer and more efficient elevators on the Mississippi River and Great Lakes, **9**.

The Pacific Northwest still has a vibrant grain export business with nine grain shipping terminals, two on Puget Sound and seven at ports along the Columbia River. More than a quarter of all U.S. grain exports and nearly half of U.S. wheat exports move through the Columbia River and Puget Sound grain terminals. The Northwest's proximity to Asian markets drives grain exports from the region. Vancouver also has a half dozen grain export terminals.

Louis Dreyfus grain terminal

It is not often that a modeler gets to design a balloon loop layout based on a prototype that is fully to scale with no selective compression, **10**. But such is the case with the FREMO module design based on the Louis Dreyfus grain terminal in downtown Portland, Oregon. (See track plan on page 31.)

First built in 1914, this grain elevator just north of the steel bridge in Portland is one of the nation's longest serving grain terminals. It was recently upgraded by Louis Dreyfus and remains very busy.

The elevator is adjacent to Union Pacific's north-south main line from California, **11**. Lying just to the north of the elevator is Albina Yard, Union Pacific's main classification yard in

Portland. Trains can continue north to Washington via trackage rights on BNSF or head east along the Columbia River. It is a busy spot as they switch power there, and yard lead switch jobs break down inbound trains and assemble outbound ones.

The FREMO module utilizes three sections to capture the facility without compression. FREMO is a module standard that allows a lot of flexibility in model design.

The loop track has a radius of about 16". The facility uses a small Trackmobile to switch the cars from the storage tracks to the unloading shed, but larger engines drop off cars at the shed lead track.

Each of three pieces of the module set are rather large. To make the sections smaller, the riverfront and ship could be omitted or built as a removable section. If transporting such big sections is an issue, the module could be built with room to spare on two smaller 3 x 4-foot modules in N scale. The module could also be incorporated into a home layout as Layout Design Elements.

The model grain elevator silos are tricky to make using the standard PVC tube technique because the prototype silos tubes overlap. You could simplify the model construction by omitting that feature and simply place the silo tubes side-by-side, but that would result in a fewer number of silos.

The Port of Beaumont is the busiest harbor in the United States for shipping military vehicles. Here, port workers under the watchful eye of U.S. Transportation Corps personnel unload Bradley Fighting Vehicles from DODX flatcars at a side-load car ramp at the port. *U.S. Army*

The 590-foot-long bulk carrier *Oriana C* takes on grain at the Port of Beaumont grain elevator. The ship holds 34,000 deadweight tonnage, a measure of how much the ship can safely carry. *Port of Beaumont*

Port of Beaumont

The track plan on page 31, based on part of the Port of Beaumont, includes a large grain elevator, a modern break bulk terminal, an aggregate loader, and an oil terminal, **12**.

The Port of Beaumont dates back to 1908, and the first docks were built in 1916. Now it is the fourth busiest port in the United States by cargo tonnage. It is also the busiest military port in the world and is headquarters for the 842nd Transportation Battalion, U.S. Army Surface Deployment & Distribution Command, which specializes in port logistics, **13** and **14**.

The port has access to the Gulf of Mexico and the Intracoastal Waterway, about 42 miles south on the Neches River.

Louis Dreyfus Commodities owns the port's grain elevator, and the Dreyfus Yard supports the grain elevator. Grain is the predominant cargo handled at the port. The elevator can accommodate 3.5 million bushels and has a loading capacity of 80,000 bushels per hour, **15**.

Kinder Morgan has a bulk terminal located between the grain elevator and Harbor Island Marine Terminal, **16**. This site handles all types of construction material, including limestone, potash, aggregate, and granite.

The port can handle project cargo and automobiles at the open wharf and on Harbor Island. The port uses a Liebherr 500 Mobile Harbor Crane.

Three Class 1 railroads, BNSF, KCS, and UP, serve the port, while Trans Global Solutions/Econo-Rail provides the port with local rail services and switching on a contract basis, **17**. Most trains entering the Port of Beaumont use the Port Interchange Yard just north of the KSC main line while the port is on the south side. Some of the track in the interchange yard prohibits the use of 6-axle locomotives.

In a typical year, the Port of Beaumont handles about 50,000

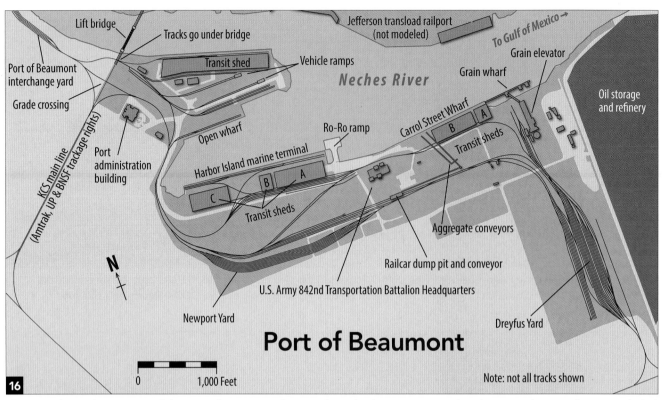

Lift bridge
Tracks go under bridge
Jefferson transload railport (not modeled)
To Gulf of Mexico →
Port of Beaumont interchange yard
Grade crossing
Transit shed
Vehicle ramps
Neches River
Grain elevator
Grain wharf
Oil storage and refinery
KCS main line (Amtrak, UP & BNSF trackage rights)
Port administration building
Open wharf
Ro-Ro ramp
Carrol Street Wharf
A
B
Transit sheds
Harbor Island marine terminal
B
A
C
Transit sheds
Aggregate conveyors
N
Railcar dump pit and conveyor
U.S. Army 842nd Transportation Battalion Headquarters
Newport Yard
Port of Beaumont
Dreyfus Yard
16
0   1,000 Feet
Note: not all tracks shown

This map shows the portions of the Port of Beaumont, from Harbor Island Marine Terminal to the grain elevator, that are included in the model railroad design.

17

Two Trans Global Solutions locomotives bring a cut of grain cars out of the staging yard just north of Beaumont Harbor. *Ghislain Gerrad*

railcars, almost a thousand a week. Of those cars, BNSF moves half, UP moves 40 percent, and KCS handles the rest. Those numbers do not count the recently constructed Jefferson Energy's transload oil terminal, a massive loop track facility located on the east bank of the Neches River that can handle petroleum unit trains.

The port completed an improvement project to reduce congestion for UP and BNSF trains entering the interchange yard via the low line under the bridge. The track plan ignores that new track and shows the UP and BNSF entering the low line under the bridge.

The layout is a walk-in design using narrow shelves. The staging tracks represent the interchange yard for the Class 1 railroads. An optional removable section allows KCS trains to enter the layout from the right-hand side as well as providing a continuous run. It also allows the KCS to interchange directly to Dreyfus Yard.

The track plan supports trains as long as 16 cars. Port of Beaumont switchers would come out of the port to the staging yards, sort the cars, and

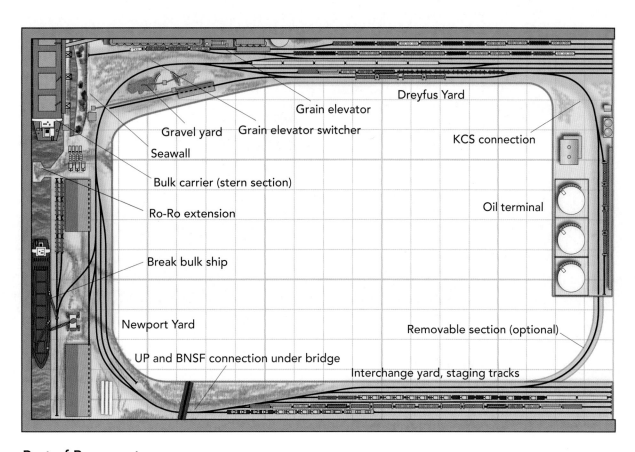

Port of Beaumont

Scale: HO
Size: 13 x 20 feet
Prototype: Beaumont, Texas

Era: 2009
Style: Shelf
Mainline run: 60 feet

Minimum radius: 30"
Turnouts: No. 6
Train length: 16 cars

Scale of plan:
5/16" = 1 foot, 12" grid

---

bring back cars consigned to the port. The port switchers work the Harbor Island Marine Terminal as well as the gravel yard and oil terminal. They drop off cars for the grain elevator as required but do not switch them into the elevator. The grain elevator has its own switch engines to shuffle cars to the unloading pit.

To save space, the plan shows only the stern of a large bulk carrier tied up at the grain wharf. Truncating the ship model simplifies the task of building it.

The U.S. Army utilizes the Harbor Island Marine Terminal to ship military vehicles. They can be unloaded at a ramp or lifted directly from the railcars using one of the port's heavy-duty cranes. Other break bulk cargo, such as windmill parts, lumber products, and rice, is sent here.

Like its prototype, this layout packs a lot of action in a modest 260 square feet.

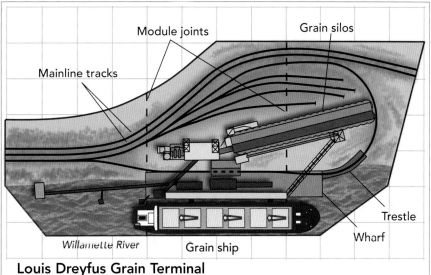

Louis Dreyfus Grain Terminal

Scale: HO
Size: 12 x 7 feet
Prototype:
Portland, Oregon
Era: 2016

Style: FREMO module
Mainline run: 12 feet
Minimum radius:
36" on main, 16" on loop
Turnouts: No. 6

Train length: 6–12 cars
Scale of plan:
3/8" = 1 foot, 12" grid

CHAPTER FOUR

Mineral terminals

CSX coal hoppers sit on the loop track at the Dominion Terminal Associates facility in Newport News, Virginia. The blue machines in the background are bucket-wheel reclaimers and stackers used to store and reclaim coal from the storage piles inside the loop.

Since the industrial revolution, people have developed a bewildering array of machines to move mineral bulk loads from the mines to users. Those machines range from simple hoppers and chutes to miles-long conveyor systems connected to massive bucket-wheel stackers and reclaimers, **1**. They also include railcar dumpers, truck dumpers, ship loaders, hoppers, and storage facilities such as stockyards, storage silos, and stockpiles. This chapter shows how these interesting devices can be incorporated into a model railroad, with a marine terminal bulk-loading operation as a focal point.

2 The Norfolk & Western's Pier 3 at Norfolk dwarfs the six-masted schooner and tramp steamer docked alongside in this early 20th century view. Steam engines pushed the wooden hoppers up a long ramp to get in position to drop coal into the dock's storage bins. Using gravity, chutes from the bins directed coal into a ship's hold. *Library of Congress*

This chapter covers minerals such as coal, iron ore, gypsum, phosphate, and aggregate in dry bulk cargoes. Grain was covered in the previous chapter. Oil and chemicals are another class of bulk cargo that can be found on marine terminals. However, the terminals for those liquid cargoes do not normally bring the railroads in close proximity to ships.

Unlike most other terminals, coal and ore marine terminals usually handle bulk materials in one-way traffic. Even if it were not so, loading and unloading requires quite different equipment, thus the respective terminals are different in design and operation.

In addition, the terminals' equipment must account for the properties of the bulk material being handled since some are heavier than others, they flow at different rates, and some, such as lump coal, are breakable. Also, when working with a ship, the machines must keep the vessel on an even keel while loading and unloading.

3 The Pennsylvania Railroad had three coal dumpers at Sandusky, Ohio. This one is a McMyler-type car dumper. It used ramps and a lifting bed to raise the hopper car high above the ship. Then the bed rotated to dump the contents into the waiting ship via a pan and loading arm. The yellow-painted cart in the foreground is a barney. *Library of Congress*

4 In this detailed photo, a McMyler-type car dumper unloads lump coal from a PRR two-bay hopper into a lake boat's fuel bunker at Sandusky, Ohio, in May 1943. Note the spilled coal on the deck and heavy weathering. *Library of Congress*

5 Modelers at the Severna Park Model Railroad Club in Severna Park, Maryland, built an operating rotary dumper for their HO scale layout. Compare this amazing model to the prototype in photo 4. *Paul Dolkos*

Ideally, they should load the entire cargo aboard without moving a vessel, and be able to handle the loaded and empty railcars to and from the machine. From a model railroader's perspective, most of those factors are determined when you select a facility to model. A model railroad designer does not need to be overly concerned with the subordinate engineering details that might affect a real facilities operation, but they are worth understanding to ensure that your models are as realistic as possible.

Bulk terminals for loading ships

All mineral bulk terminals have three main functional components: loading or unloading machines, material-handling systems, and storage areas. On a model railroad, the process starts when loaded railcars arrive at a port terminal. The railcars must be

unloaded, either directly to the ship or to a storage area.

The pier with a trestle and pocket system was the first of the dedicated bulk mineral ship-loading terminals. The ore pier at Two Harbors, Minnesota, built before World War I is an example. This pier was 1,368 feet long and 56 feet wide, and it carried a trestle 80 feet high with car tracks on top. Iron ore ports on Lake Superior and Lake Michigan all had similar piers, although variations were possible, such as the loop pier at Taconite Harbor (for more on that port, see my earlier book, *Mid-Size Track Plans for Realistic Layouts*). Port operators built similar trestle and pocket piers for coal, gravel, and other minerals, **2**.

In a trestle and pocket system, locomotive engines shove cars from a railroad marshaling yard over pockets on each side of the pier. The cars dump their loads into the pockets using the

hopper doors on the car bottoms. The pier acts as a transit shed as the bins hold the material until the ship docks alongside the pier.

By adjusting the type of material dropped in the bin, terminal technicians could blend the material to a user's specifications. When modeling a trestle and bin system, you can simulate the blending operation by giving each car a waybill to a particular pocket. Model train operators would have to spot each car over a particular pocket. This adds complexity and interest to the switching job in what otherwise could be a straightforward and uninteresting task of spotting cars over bins.

The pockets, cars, and ship hatches all have to be of corresponding dimensions to align and register correctly. If the ship's loading hatches are not aligned, the process is less efficient as the crews would have to move the ship during loading. At the

The former Western Maryland coal export pier in Port Covington, Maryland, had both a McMyler (right background) and a rotary car dumper (left foreground). Conveyors transported coal from the rotary dumper to a movable loading arm farther out on the pier (just visible left of the McMyler dumper). *Library of Congress*

turn of the 19th century, most lake ore-loading facilities had loading chutes spaced every 12 feet. Thus, lake vessels carrying ore, coal, or grain had hatches spaced 24 feet apart. A lake vessel has many more hatches than an ocean vessel of equal length. Ship designers continue to use this pattern today, even with modern lake vessels.

Vessel speeds are not as important on the Great Lakes, as lake ports are not as far apart as ocean ports. For Great Lakes boats, cargo capacity is more important than speed. Therefore, ship designers of lake boats have favored bluff bows over streamlined bows and boxy hulls. Those hulls are easy to scratchbuild, especially as waterline models, although whaleback lake boats are an exception. (See chapter 10 for more on building ship models.) Great Lakes shipbuilders also had to consider the size of the locks of the Great Lakes and the

Saint Lawrence Seaway system when designing ships.

While trestle and bin piers remained in ore service, car dumpers replaced the trestle and bins for coal and other bulk materials when the McMyler Corporation introduced them around 1910. A car dumper avoids some of the problems associated with bottom-dump railcars. First, the sloping bottoms of traditional hoppers can leave some coal inside a railcar even after unloading, usually due to clumped or frozen material. Second, bottom-dump railcars have the potential to spill their contents onto the tracks, especially if there are any imperfections in the door seals. Third, bottom-dump railcars often have a lengthier unloading process.

A typical McMyler car dumper installation would have classification and car storage yards for loads and empties, a thawing house for frozen

loads, and one or more car dumpers. Locomotives would set a full railcar at the base of the pier's ramp. There, a barney, a mechanism that grabs the car underneath or by the coupler, would move the car to the unloader at the top of the ramp, **3**. Upon reaching the unloader, the barney releases the car and then overhead clamps grab the car. The device raises the clamped car vertically above an unloader pan, where it turns 120 degrees and spills the material out onto the pan, usually accompanied by a huge cloud of dust, **4**.

The pan funnels the coal into a chute leading to a waiting boat or barge. Trimmers on the boat spread the coal evenly so the boat doesn't list or overturn. The unloader returns the car to the normal vertical position at the ramp and releases it. It rolls onto a kickback trestle, which extends out into the harbor. It resembles a roller coaster in construction; the far end of

35

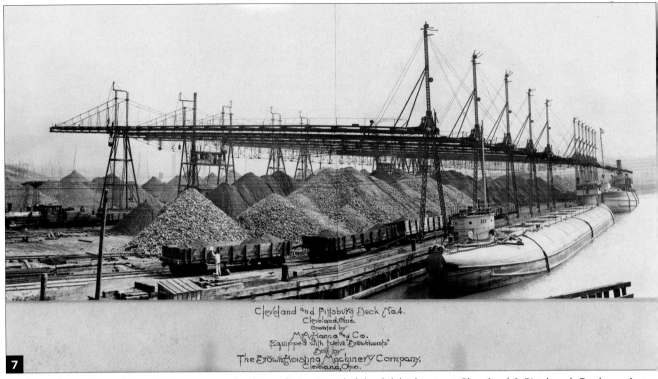

7

Twelve early versions of Brownhoist cranes unload two distinctive whaleback lake boats at Cleveland & Pittsburgh Dock no. 4 at Whiskey Island, Cleveland. These cranes would later be replaced by Hulett unloaders. *Library of Congress*

the trestle curves up into the air where gravity slows down and stops the car. There, it changes tracks using a spring switch and then travels toward land using another downward sloping track.

On some installations, the dumper was on the land side and not on the pier. The car dumper would feed a hopper connected to the pier via conveyor belts. Usually the hopper would have additional conveyors to bring coal that wasn't immediately going to be loaded onto the ship to a stockpile.

In 1924, Heyl & Patterson improved the car dumper with the rotary car dumper, which quickly became the industry standard for unloading cars. (The Severna Park Model Railroad Club has an operating dumper of this type on their layout, **5**.)

The rotary dumper holds a railcar in place inside the dumper with clamps, and the entire mechanism rotates so that the car is nearly upside down, **6**. The car remains on the same elevation as the dumper rotates the cars on the axis of the couplers, so it can quickly return to position once the rotation is complete.

Later railroads developed rotary couplers, which allowed cars to rotate and dump their loads without being uncoupled from one another. In a tandem dumper, two railcars at a time can be dumped. A rotary dumper can unload one car in as little as 35 seconds and dump up to 5,000 tons per hour, or 10,000 tons per hour in tandem configuration. Now, manufacturers offer triple and quadruple rotary dumpers to enhance productivity.

Bulk terminals for unloading ships

While grain elevators had marine legs, for ore and coal the comparable invention was the McMyler whirler, which was a revolving jib crane that lifted a 1-ton bucket of ore from a ship to a railroad car. The revolving derrick had two buckets. As one was being loaded by a shovel in the hold, the other would ride up above the deck. Although clever, the whirlers had limited capacity.

In 1880, Alexander Brown of Cleveland invented the Brownhoist crane, which revolutionized the bulk material shipping industry. Brown designed a cantilevered crane, rigged with wire rope, that conveyed a 1½-ton clamshell bucket to and from a ship's hold, removing the cargo to the stockpile or to a waiting railroad car. His hoist, first set up on Lake Erie docks, reduced transportation costs and greatly shortened the turnaround time of vessels. By 1900, about 75 percent of ore shipped on the Great Lakes was handled by Brownhoist equipment, **7**.

Another unloading machine was the traveling bridge crane, manufactured by Hoover & Mason Company of Chicago around the same time. It had a heavy automatic grab bucket, with a spread of 18 feet, that was capable of filling itself with any grade ore. The closing motion was very peculiar, as a downward biting motion of the blades affected penetration and was followed by a horizontal scraping to complete closure. Also in this class of unloader was the Mead Morrison rig, a much taller version of the traveling bridge crane.

Clamshell grabs are still in wide use around the world, **8**. Some bulk ships have cranes and grabs built on their hulls for use in ports without unloading facilities (such as the Oldendorff bulk carrier in photo 20).

The Hulett "grasshopper" unloader, developed by Frank E. Hulett in 1898, was the next improved device, **9**. It consisted of a massive frame, or walking beam, whose front end rested on the face of the dock and the back end on a slightly raised concrete wall. A carriage on the frame moved backward and forward over the ore trough. At the outer end of the walking beam were legs that reached down into the hold. One man operated the walking beam mechanism from a position inside the leg, so he would ride it up and down.

Weighing hoppers were located underneath the main frame and along the bottom. The operator elevated the bucket, loaded with 15–20 tons, clear of the vessel, so the carriage could run back on the main frame until the bucket was over a weighing hopper or an ore trough, and the load was released.

A cable ran alongside each track under the hoppers so an operator could move the railcars. The operator pulled a lever on the mechanical clamp attached to the train and moved the car or the train half a car length for the next load.

For many years, they were the fastest shoreside unloaders in the world. There were about 80 Hulett unloaders built in several variants across the United States, with most working on the Great Lakes, although one unloaded garbage barges in New York.

Walthers produced a model of a Hulett unloader in HO scale, thus simplifying the task of including them on a layout. Modelers in other scales must resort to scratchbuilding, **10**.

A self-unloader has mechanical conveyor equipment for unloading its cargo built into its hull, **11**. The advantage of this type of boat is that it can call at ports not equipped with unloading cranes. The disadvantages, as compared to a conventional ship, are a higher capital cost, lower carrying capacity as the self-unloading conveyor system takes space, and more downtime since, if the unloader is down, the ship is also down.

Stacking and reclaimers

Unloading from ship to freight cars is less common than from ship to stockpiles. A stockpile at a bulk material terminal serves as the reservoir for bulk

Clamshell buckets on traveling cranes, generically called *grabs*, are still in service. In 2015, Rukert Terminals used grabs to unload road salt from the bulk carrier *AP Sveti Vlaho* to a string of dump trucks. In earlier times, railcars would have been used instead of trucks.

These Hulett unloaders are seen at Whiskey Island, Ohio. Walthers offers a nice kit of these unloaders in HO scale. *Library of Congress*

Monroe Stewart built these N scale Hulett unloaders from scratch as no commercial kits were available.

The *John Munson* is a typical lake boat with a self-unloading system. Here it is dropping coal at a power plant on the Rouge River in 2008. The boat was built in 1952 as part of U.S. Steel's fleet.

The Duluth, South Shore & Atlantic Railway wooden ore dock in Marquette, Michigan, is seen here in 1911. It would be replaced with a steel and concrete version in 1931.
Library of Congress

materials. Terminals put coal, ore, gravel, sand, and other materials in stockpiles for storage. Because navigation is closed during winter on the Great Lakes, industries that use the lakes must stockpile bulk materials.

A reclaimer is a large machine used to recover bulk material, such as ore or coal, from a stockpile. Reclaimers normally travel on a rail between stockpiles in the stockyard. Bucket-wheel reclaimers use a rotating wheel equipped with buckets to remove material from the pile they are reclaiming (see photo 1). Scraper reclaimers use a series of scrapers on a chain to reclaim the material.

A stacker piles bulk material such as limestone, ore, or coal onto a stockpile. They normally travel on a rail between stockpiles in the stockyard. A stacker can usually move in two directions: horizontally along the rail and vertically by raising and lowering its boom. Raising and lowering the boom minimizes dust by reducing the distance that material needs to fall to the top of the stockpile. Some stackers can rotate the boom. This allows a single stacker to form two stockpiles, one on either side of the conveyor.

Iron ore trade

In 1844, surveyor William Burt discovered iron ore in Michigan's Upper Peninsula when the iron in the ground disturbed his magnetic compasses. Other entrepreneurs developed his and other finds through the early 1850s. They initially tried producing iron locally, as shipping was difficult. Early ore transport used mule teams, plank roads, sleighs (in winter), and barrels to load it on schooners. Schooners required transshipment to portage the rapids between Lake Superior and Lake Huron, but the costs proved prohibitive.

In spite of the winter and difficult transport, miners continued to develop the rich deposits. In 1855, railroads reached the area, and the Soo Locks opened. Shipping by rail and sailboat became simplified, and the volume of shipped ore increased, with the first year seeing 1,447 tons on various brigs and schooners.

The town of Marquette built the first dock specifically for the ore trade in 1857. It was flat rather than elevated, and vessels were loaded by wheelbarrow. In 1862, Marquette installed an additional wooden dock, this time featuring an elevated railway trestle so ore jennies could discharge ore into pockets. Following that, the Cleveland Iron Mining Company built a new ore dock in Marquette and then extended it in 1872, giving it a total of 83 schooner pockets. Marquette remained the only port on Lake Superior that shipped iron ore until 1876, **12**.

Miners developed additional ranges in Michigan, especially the Gogebic and Menominee. To ship the newly discovered ore, other Michigan ports, such as Ashland and Escanaba, built ore docks.

In 1931, railroads built another iron ore dock in Marquette. A concrete and steel frame replaced the wooden dock. It was 1,200 feet long, 75 feet high, and 60 feet wide. Four railroad tracks ran across the top, and there was storage space inside the bottom concrete part for 60,000 tons of iron ore.

There are three iron ranges in northern Minnesota: the Cuyuna, the Vermilion, and the Mesabi. Miners started extracting ore in this area in 1902. They proved to be some of the richest iron ore deposits in the world and are still mined today. A maze of track and an array of ore docks help transship the ore to steel mills on the southern Great Lakes. In 1922, these mines shipped nearly 300 million tons of ore in one season, **13**. (The term *season* is used instead of *year* since the Great Lakes freeze in the winter and lake shipping halts.) Nearly all the ore mined in these ranges goes first by rail to a harbor on Lake Michigan or Lake Superior, where it is loaded on ore-carrying boats that transport it either down Lake Michigan to Chicago or Gary, or through Lake Huron and Lake Erie to ports farther south. For most of the ore, even these lower lake ports are not ultimate destinations, and another haul by rail is required to take it to blast furnaces.

Walthers produced a modular plastic kit that accurately depicted

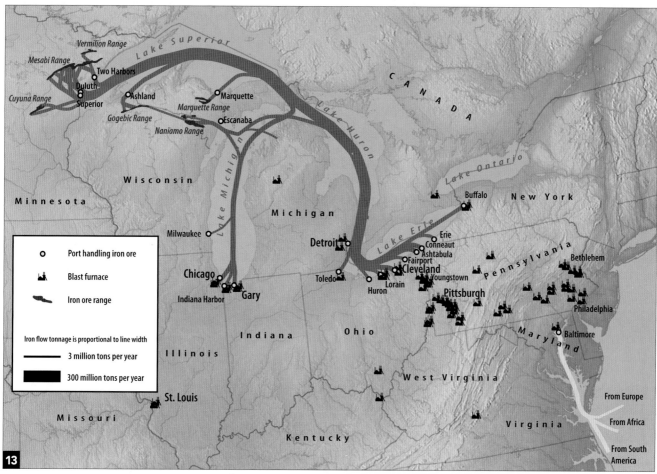

The map shows the maritime flow of iron ore in the United States in 1922. The orange bands show Lake Superior iron ore. The yellow line shows iron ore flows to Sparrows Point, near Baltimore, from overseas sources. The brown areas indicate the ranges where the iron ore originates. Also indicated on the map are the approximate location of blast furnaces in operation at that time. Today, the flow pattern in the Great Lakes is similar except that only a handful of blast furnaces still operate in the United States, and most of the Michigan mines are closed. The Sparrows Point mill in Baltimore is also now closed. *(compiled from various sources, primarily the Lake Superior Iron Ore Association)*

Jeff Otto has one of the largest model railroads that focuses on iron ore shipments. It includes a large area that depicts the Port of Duluth, Minnesota. He built these two ore dock models using multiple Walthers ore dock kits. The docks look great with strings of short ore cars set over the bins and ships alongside. *Jeff Otto*

Ken Larsen's layout features a waterfront steel mill that receives ore and coal delivered by ore boats. He scratchbuilt the traveling crane. *Ken Larsen*

At the Consol Coal terminal in Canton, Maryland, Conrail engines pull coal trains through the rotary dumper.

The Consol terminal has two rail-mounted combination stacker-reclaimers. The bucket-wheel excavators dig into the coal pile to transfer the coal to a conveyor that sends it to a ship. The conveyors can reverse direction to act as stackers.

a typical Great Lakes ore dock. By using multiple kits, you can build prototypically sized ore docks without having to scratchbuild, as Jeff Otto did on his large, double-deck iron ore themed railroad, **14**. His layout includes two large ore docks as well as two large piers for grain and general cargo.

Coal trade

Model railroaders tend to think of coal as a single commodity, but it is much more complex than that. The coal industry classifies it in four general ranks based on its properties. From lowest to highest rank, they are lignite, sub-bituminous, bituminous, and anthracite. Lower rank coals have less carbon, more moisture, and lower calorific values.

The industry further classifies coal as either thermal or metallurgical. Thermal coal is lower in carbon content and calorific value but higher in moisture value. It is the world's most abundant fossil fuel and is primarily used to produce energy. Metallurgical coal is less abundant than thermal coal and is primarily used in the production of coke, which is an important part of the integrated steel mill process, **15**.

Coal can also be shipped in various forms, including slurry or coke, and in various sizes of loose bulk such as nut, egg, lump, pea, and breeze (powder). Users specify what type and grade of coal they want. The coal companies sort and blend their coal to meet a user's needs. They can do that at the mine or at the coal export terminal. Many terminals use their stackers, reclaimers, and a system of conveyors to blend the different coal types during loading or unloading.

Metallurgical grade coal dominated U.S. exports in the past. The history of U.S. coal exporting begins in the late 1800s, when small quantities were shipped to Canada and the east coast of South America. European demand for U.S. coal began by the turn of the century and increased steadily up to World War I. In 1917, the United States exported approximately 24 million tons to foreign buyers. By 1920, 38 million

A complex arrangement of conveyors route coal in various directions as needed.

A large bulk carrier takes on coal in this aerial photo of the complete Consol Coal loop. At right are finger piers formerly served by the Canton Railroad, now largely unused. *John Kellog, IAN Image Library (ian.umces.edu/imagelibrary)*

tons left U.S. ports, with 22 million tons bound for non-Canadian points.

Immediately following World War II, the United States emerged as a major coal supplier with export levels ranging from 69 million tons in 1947 to 76 million tons in 1957. Following that year, coal leaving U.S. ports was always less than the 1957 totals, until 1980, when almost 90 million tons were exported.

The United States is still an exporter of coal. In 2012, 12 percent of U.S. coal production was exported, accounting for approximately 7 percent of coal imported by other countries.

The United States imports about 1 percent of the coal it uses, mostly to power plants in the country's eastern and southern regions, where it is cheaper to bring coal in by sea from South America than transport it from

coal mines in northern and western states.

The United States exported 74 million tons and imported 11 million tons in 2015. Now, about one-quarter of exported coal is steam coal.

U.S. coal exports are mainly shipped from six districts: Hampton Roads, Mobile, New Orleans, San Francisco, Seattle, and Baltimore. Baltimore has two coal export facilities arranged in

Two large bulk carriers take on coal at the Dominion Terminal Associates Newport News export terminal in 2015. The Kinder Morgan loop is just visible in the background.

Concrete silos connected by conveyors comprise the stacker-reclaimer in the Kinder Morgan coal loop at Newport News. The loops use tandem rotary dumpers.

loops. (Photos **16–19** show the Consol Coal loop facility in Canton.) Tampa overtook Mobile to become the largest recipient of coal imports in 2015.

Coal investors built two modern coal terminals on the West Coast in the last two decades of the 20th century. One at the Port of Portland failed a few years after opening in the 1980s. A consortium in Los Angeles was aware of that failure, but went ahead and built one of the finest coal terminals in North America, the only U.S. terminal capable of loading a 275,000-deadweight-ton vessel. It was commissioned in 1997, but it stopped shipping coal in 2003 mostly due to weak sales to Asia as well as environmental concerns.

CSX Peninsula Subdivision

The C&O railroad traditionally relied on coal shipments for a large part of its profitability. From Appalachian mines, it shipped coal west to marine terminals at Presque Isle near Toledo and east to Newport News on the Peninsula Subdivision in Virginia.

The layout design depicts the Peninsula Subdivision in the modern time period, now under CSX control, **20**. The export terminal formerly used trestle and bins, and later, McMyler dumpers. In 1983, the terminal operators replaced the McMyler dumpers with a set of two coal loops utilizing rotary dumpers and rotary couplers, **21**. This N scale layout

features one of these loops on Pier XI, now operated by Kinder Morgan for CSX. This layout is perfect for model railroaders that like to run long coal trains.

Coal loops are space hogs, and the layout reflects that, **22**. The loop design permits loads-in/empties-out operation for the rotary dumper. The double-track loops allow operation in two different manners. The first technique would use the loops without reversing the empties. One track would have loaded trains going counter clockwise, while empties use the other loop's track in a clockwise direction. This creates a loads-in/ empties-out type of operation.

An overview of the coal loops at Newport News. The surge silos at the water's edge hold the coal being transferred to the ships.

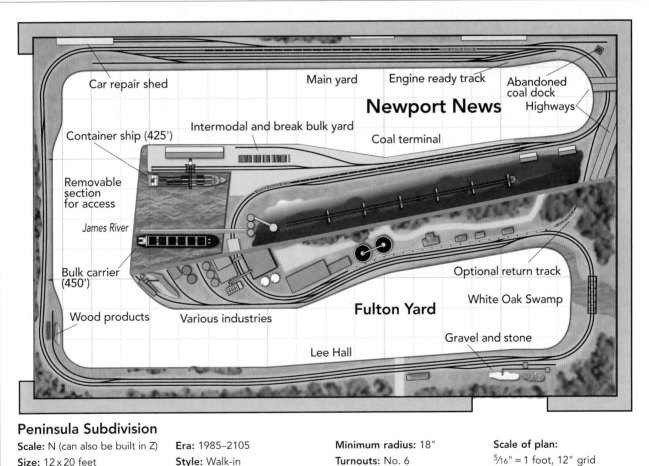

Peninsula Subdivision

Scale: N (can also be built in Z)	**Era:** 1985–2105	**Minimum radius:** 18"	**Scale of plan:**
Size: 12 x 20 feet	**Style:** Walk-in	**Turnouts:** No. 6	⁵⁄₁₆" = 1 foot, 12" grid
Prototype: CSX	**Mainline run:** 110 feet	**Train length:** 24 cars	

Alternatively, empty trains that arrive in Fulton Yard from Newport News would stop. Their engines would swap ends of the train. Then the train would return to the Newport News yard using the partially hidden return track.

The plan includes the modest container and break bulk terminal at the port. In addition, there are several industries in Fulton Yard and along the main line to justify running a local freight. But the main action is running coal trains to and from the port.

The layout depicts two ships at the dock. To improve access for maintenance of the track in the coal loop, the James River section could be removable.

This layout would be easy to convert to Z scale, as its emphasis on running trains is perfect for a Z scale layout. The track plan would remain the same, perhaps with a few additional yard tracks. The structures, ships, and curve radii would not change. The large radii in Z scale would make the layout look and run well.

1

CHAPTER FIVE

Railroad ferries and car float terminals

Paul Dolkos scratchbuilt this transfer bridge and car float on his Port of Baltimore HO scale layout, which combines prototype elements in a freelance design. *Paul Dolkos*

The previous chapters discussed marine terminals where railroads transfer their cargo to and from freight cars and ships. Sometimes railroads place a railcar on a ship without unloading it contents. While stevedores can load a whole car on a conventional ship using booms and cranes, specialized ships designed to carry railcars are much faster to load and unload. These specialized ships are either railroad ferries or railroad car floats (car ferries and car floats for short).

A car ferry is a ship that has railway tracks on one or more decks that can carry railroad cars. Car ferries have steam or diesel engines onboard to provide the ship with power. Conversely, a railroad car float is an unpowered barge with rail tracks mounted on its deck. Tugboats move the car floats, usually from along the side of the car float since they load and unload from the bow. Both ferries and car floats use transfer bridges and piers with aprons to connect the onboard tracks to shoreside tracks, although not interchangeably.

Car floats and, to a lesser extent, car ferries have fascinated model railroaders for decades. There is something innately interesting in transferring a freight car to a barge in a model operation, probably due to the specialized equipment and the variety of operation from normal over-the-track running. Many modelers build car floats, transfer bridges, aprons, and associated yards, **1**. A smaller number model railroad ferries, probably because they tend to be larger and more difficult to build. This chapter covers the history, equipment, and operation of car floats and ferries in the United States and Canada in prototype and model form.

Railroad car ferries

The first railroad ferry operation in the United States began in 1836 at the Philadelphia, Wilmington & Baltimore crossing of the Susquehanna River in Maryland. Southbound trains stopped at Perryville, Maryland, at the wide mouth of the Susquehanna River where it empties into Chesapeake Bay, **2**. The crews detached the cars from the engine and rolled them onto tracks on top of the railroad ferry *Susquehanna*, prior to December 1854, and on the larger *Maryland* after that. Passengers gathered on the lower deck. Upon reaching the opposite shore at Harve de Grace, the cars were attached to another engine, and the passengers reentered the cars. The ferry remained in operation until 1866, when it was replaced by a bridge hurriedly constructed during the Civil War but not finished until the war was over.

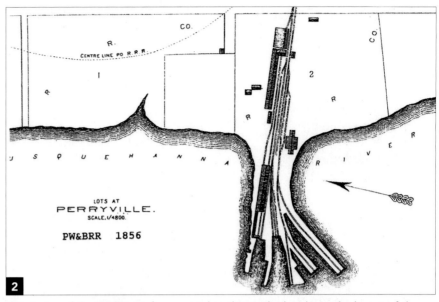

No photos of the PW&B car ferry exist, but this track plan shows the layout of the tracks at Perryville, Maryland, the first car ferry operation in the United States.

In the next 50 years, railroads built and operated hundreds of car ferries on rivers and bays across the United States and Canada. On the Mississippi River, one of the notable examples was the Illinois Central's *Pelican*. It plied the "father of waters" between Helena, Arkansas, and Lula, Mississippi, carrying both freight cars and locomotives. Built in 1902, the side-wheel paddle steamer ran until 1960.

The bays and rivers near San Francisco had many active car ferries during the steam and transition eras. One of the largest ever built was the *Solano*. Like the *Pelican*, it was a side-wheel paddleboat that operated across the 1-mile-wide Carquinez Strait between Benicia and Port Costa. The Central Pacific built it in 1878 and operated it to shuttle entire trains on the Central Pacific transcontinental line to and from the San Francisco Bay area. Once the ferry was in service, the CP rerouted the transcontinental line to it from the original course over Altamont Pass. At 424 feet long and 116 feet wide, the *Solano* was the largest car ferry built at the time. It could carry a complete passenger train or 48 freight cars and a locomotive. The CP built a second ferry, the *Contra Costa*, as a sister ship in 1914. It was slightly larger than *Solano*, and remains the largest rail ferryboat ever built. It remained in service until 1930, when

the Southern Pacific built a bridge over the strait making them unnecessary.

The Oakland Long Wharf, later known as the Southern Pacific Mole, was a massive railroad wharf and ferry pier along the east shore of San Francisco Bay in Oakland. It anchored the westernmost terminus of the first transcontinental railroad. It was a wooden wharf over 2 miles long to take the tracks beyond the shallow mudflats along the shore of East Bay until they extended into water that was deep enough to accommodate passenger and car ferries. Initially, Central Pacific trains on the Oakland side exchanged passengers and goods with ferries from San Francisco. The wooden wharf was vulnerable to teredo worms (also known as termites of the sea) and required constant maintenance. So between 1879 and 1882, the railroad filled in part of the wharf with rocks and dirt to create a mole.

The Southern Pacific took over the mole around 1882. Under its control, the mole became one of the busiest stations in the United States. In 1920, the mole handled 763 mainline and suburban passenger trains in 24 hours. Construction of the Bay Bridge reduced the traffic that the mole handled. In the 1960s, work crews demolished the mole to make room for an expansion of the Port of Oakland container terminal.

3

Animated doors and full lighting highlight this model of the SP Oakland Mole on Pliny Holt's N scale layout.

The late Pliny Holt built a highly detailed model of the mole set in the SP era for his N scale model railroad. His model included animated doors and full lights, **3**.

The Ann Arbor Railroad, Grand Trunk, and Pere Marquette, which became part of Chesapeake & Ohio in 1947, ran railroad car ferries across Lake Michigan. At their peak, car ferries sailed across Lake Michigan on up to 15 different ferry routes.

Transporting freight cars across Lake Michigan grew out of the need to bypass the congested rail yards in Chicago. It could take a week or longer for a freight car to transit through the congested yards and transfer runs from railroad to railroad in Chicago. Lake Michigan car ferries cut that time to a few days, with the actual sailing taking less than 7 hours.

Ann Arbor was the pioneer in Lake Michigan car ferry service, operating three routes from a hub in Frankfort, Michigan, to three ports in Wisconsin: Sturgeon Bay, Kewaunee, and Milwaukee. The service lasted until 1982. The Grand Trunk Milwaukee Ferry Company, a subsidiary of Grand Trunk Western, ran a single route from Muskegon, Michigan, to Milwaukee, which lasted until 1978. Pere Marquette/Chesapeake & Ohio operated the most railroad car ferries on Lake Michigan. Pere Marquette car ferries sailed three routes from a hub in Ludington, Michigan, to Milwaukee, Manitowoc, and Kewaunee. (One C&O ferry still operates today for automobiles and passengers but not for railroad cars.)

The ferries used powerful coal-burning steam engines. They needed the power to sometimes break through ice since the ferries ran year-round.

All the boats utilized stern gates for loading railcars, which the U.S. Coast Guard required. They also used jacking rails to secure the 24–34 cars typically carried on the decks. The pair of jacking rails were 25" outside the railroad tracks embedded in a ship's deck. Crewmen used screw jacks to lift the railroad car bodies off their trucks. Then they secured the car bodies to the jacking rails with chains. As a result, the ships had large crews of 50–60 men, much larger than a comparable train crew for the number of cars carried.

The late Arnt Gerritsen's Ann Arbor Railroad Third Subdivision HO scale model railroad included a wonderful depiction of the Frankfort ferry docks, **4**. His layout included two ferry slips and three ferries set parallel to a large freight yard. During an operating session, operators would switch cars on and off ferries in accordance with prototype practices.

From 1915 until 1935, the Florida East Coast Railway operated a subsidiary car ferry service (Florida East Coast Car Ferry) between Key

West and Havana. The FEC's line to Key West from Miami was an engineering marvel with several very long bridges and causeways, **5**. Alas, a 1935 hurricane completely destroyed the section that ran through the Florida Keys, although some bridges survived. So the FEC moved its U.S. terminal to Port Everglades near Fort Lauderdale. Three steam-powered car ferries operated in regular service between the United States and Cuba up to the beginning of World War II. The Navy requisitioned the ferries for use during the war.

After World War II, a new company, The West India Fruit and Steamship Company, took over the car ferry service from the FEC and moved the terminal to the Port of Palm Beach, **6**. The service was successful, and three more ships were added to the fleet. WIF&SS acted as both a railroad and a steamship line, calling the service "The Superior All-Rail Route to Cuba." Company freight cars were painted with a unique steamship logo. Shippers could send freight from anywhere in North America to Cuba without having to transfer it from the cars. Ferries operated from 1946 until 1960, when the United States broke off diplomatic relations and enacted an embargo with Cuba.

Seatrain Lines, the operating name for the Over-Seas Shipping Company, took a different approach to shipping railcars by sea. Its ships did not use ramps to load the three decks with freight cars. Instead, a heavy-duty crane loaded the railcars onto cradles on elevators located midship, **7**. The cradles distributed the cars to different decks and tracks, which helped make the ships more seaworthy as they did not have vulnerable gates on the bow or stern.

Seatrain initiated service between ports in the United States and Havana in December 1928 aboard the specially designed *Seatrain*, later renamed *Seatrain New Orleans*. It was capable of carrying 95 fully loaded railcars. The company built two similar, but larger, ships with greater railcar capacity in 1932, two more in 1939, and two again in 1951.

Arnt Gerritsen scratchbuilt the ferry and transfer bridge on his HO scale layout that depicted the Ann Arbor ferry docks in Frankfort, Michigan. *Matt Kosic*

Cal Winters' layout depicts the FEC from Miami to Key West and includes several of the long bridges and the ferry terminal at Key West. *Paul Dolkos*

Seatrain's U.S. terminal was located in Hoboken, New Jersey. Seatrain owned the Hoboken Manufacturers Railroad that connected its facility to other railroads. They used small gas mechanical Whitcomb or GE diesel-electric locomotives for switching, which created an interesting spectacle of tiny locomotives pushing freight cars next to the 470-foot-long ships.

During World War II, the U.S. Navy requisitioned Seatrain's ships, though some also served under lease. They participated in several combat operations. One hazardous emergency mission required the *Seatrain Texas* to travel unescorted with a load of tanks to North Africa, relying on its 18-knot speed to get through. The tanks made it to participate in the Battle of El Alamein, a turning point in the war.

In 1951, Seatrain ceased operations to and from Cuba. In 1953, Seatrain sold its operating authority to trade between the United States and Cuba to the West India Fruit and Steamship Company, along with its first ship, *Seatrain New Orleans*. In 1958, Seatrain abandoned moving railcars and switched to containers.

6

Two West India Fruit and Steamship Company car ferries are docked at the Port of Palm Beach. A U.S. Navy warship can be seen in the foreground. (The Port of Palm Beach is a compact terminal, which is discussed more in chapter 7.) *Port of Palm Beach*

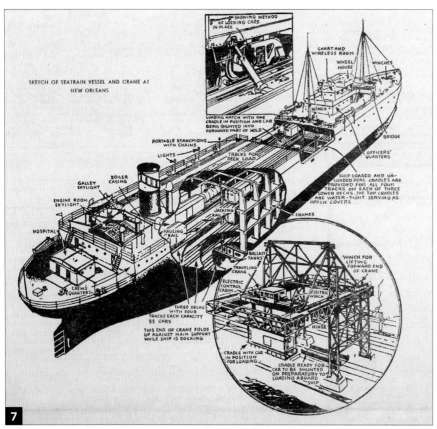

SKETCH OF SEATRAIN VESSEL AND CRANE AT NEW ORLEANS

7

This cutaway drawing of a typical Seatrain ferry shows the unusual means of loading railcars in the midship section. *Classic Trains, spring 2011*

There are a few railcar ferries still in operation in the United States. The Central Gulf operates a car ferry between the Port of Mobile, Alabama, and the Port of Coatzacoalcos in Veracruz, Mexico. It began operation in 2000 out of Mobile. In 2004, the railroad moved its American port to New Orleans, but that facility was heavily damaged by Hurricane Katrina in 2005. In 2007, the Alabama State Port Authority constructed a new, state-of-the-art $19 million rail ferry terminal at the Port of Mobile. The railroad operates two double-deck rail ferries, each capable of carrying 115 railcars, up to four times a week. The CGR transports approximately 10,000 railcars annually.

The Alaska Railroad is connected to the rest of the North American rail system only by train ferries. The Alaska Railroad runs its own ferries from Whittier, Alaska, to Seattle. The Canadian National operates its AquaTrain between Whittier and Prince Rupert, British Columbia.

Railroad car floats

Railroad car float development happened in parallel with car ferries. While car ferries were oriented on moving whole trains and acting as waterborne bridges, car floats were more involved in the freight delivery and distribution process. Railroads were intimately involved in car float operations, many having fleets of tugboats, car floats, station floats, and various barges. In addition, railroads maintained shoreside yards ranging from massive classification yards to tiny, isolated pocket terminals with no railroad access other than the car float.

General Herman Haupt of the United States Military Railroad (USMRR) developed the first railroad car float. It operated on the Potomac River during the American Civil War to support the Union's campaign to take Richmond in 1862. His innovation required modified barges and new transfer bridges at Alexandria and Aquia Landing. He designed and oversaw the construction of the unprecedented car floats and transfer bridges.

The floats consisted of two large-sized Schuylkill barges, across which were placed long timbers to support eight tracks arranged laterally, not longitudinally, **8**. USMRR crews used the transfer bridges in Alexandria to run eight loaded cars on the floats. The transfer bridge could only handle three cars at a time, so the barge had to be repositioned at least twice during a full loading. A steam tug towed the car float 60 miles to Aquia Landing. There, other railroad crews unloaded the barges by pulling the cars. They then forwarded the cars without the break of bulk along the rebuilt line of the Richmond, Fredericksburg & Potomac to various locations to serve the Union Army. The float remained in operation for about six months until the army destroyed it when it retreated north for the Gettysburg campaign. The car float was reactivated in 1864 from Alexandria to City Point to support the Petersburg campaign.

Soon after the war, other railroads began to establish car floats across the continent where water obstacles made laying tracks inconvenient. Canadian railroads used car floats to reach remote locations on inland lakes of British Columbia. Many of those served isolated pulp and paper mills. Bruce Barney models one of these operations on his double-deck HO scale layout. His version of the Canadian Pacific Boundary Division during 1968 to 1973 includes the Lake Slocan car float. He uses an ingenious, linear actuator to lift the layout sections with the car float scene from one level of his layout to another, **9**. The upper level simulates the isolated branch.

Lake Ontario also hosted several car float operations, including some that went between the United States to Canada.

The Southern Pacific had the only direct rail line to the San Francisco peninsula. It operated ferries but no car floats in San Francisco Bay. But several other railroads, including narrow gauge lines, used car floats to serve the San Francisco peninsula and bay. The State Harbor Belt Railroad in San Francisco used three-rail track to serve both standard and narrow gauge

In this HO scale diorama, a steam tug pushes a USMRR car float toward the transfer bridge at Alexandria. I built this diorama of the first-ever car float operation for the Alexandria City Museum, where it is on display.

Bruce Barney uses this clever linear actuator to lift the whole section of benchwork that contains his Lake Slocan car float scene from one level of his layout to another.

traffic coming off those floats. Most of the narrow gauge car floats were abandoned after the San Francisco earthquake in 1906.

Since the Santa Fe had no direct rail connection, it used several car floats and a fleet of three tugs to serve the peninsula and several other routes on the bay. The Santa Fe Alice Street Yard in Oakland was a pocket terminal that Santa Fe served only by car float, although the SP also had a rail connection to the area.

The Western Pacific also shuttled car floats across the bay using two steam tugs and three car floats. One

of its two tugs, the *Bouge*, sunk in a collision with a freighter in 1939. The WP replaced it with another steam tug. In 1957, the WP replaced the steam tugs and car floats with a single diesel-powered ferry, the *Las Plumas*. It ran until 1978, when a non-railroad user bought it. The WP's steam tug *Hercules* has been preserved at the San Francisco Maritime National Historical Park.

On the east coast of the United States, car floats operated in most major cities, although they were most numerous in Chesapeake Bay and New York Harbor.

Seen from Brooklyn, this view of the New York waterfront shows an incredible variety of steamships, schooners, tugs, and barges. The tall building in the background is the Singer Building, the tallest building in New York during 1908–1909. *Library of Congress*

Tim Warris built this portable model of the CNJ Bronx terminal. To emulate the prototype, Tim had to handlay some of the most complex trackwork ever built on a model railroad. *Tim Warris*

In Baltimore at the upper end of the Chesapeake Bay, the B&O and Western Maryland operated car floats. Their primary purpose was to reach locations that would have otherwise required complicated trips around the perimeter of the bay. Sometimes the shippers used the car floats to obtain a favorable shipping rate, as using a car float could be less expensive than an all-rail rate in that era of highly regulated freight rates.

In the Hampton Roads area of the Chesapeake Bay, several car floats operated. The Brooke Avenue Yard was an isolated pocket terminal in Norfolk, Virginia, served by the Chesapeake & Ohio via car float. Though it was surrounded by N&W railroad tracks, there was no land rail connection. The C&O tugs brought cars to Brooke Avenue from Newport News on the opposite side of the James River, where the C&O had massive freight yards.

The C&O car floats were 370 feet long and could hold 27 40-foot freight cars. The floats' steel hull design included a central superstructure with a smokestack. However, the floats were unpowered, and the stacks were exhausts for the powered steering system only. The C&O also had several tugs painted in its company colors of blue and gold.

The track plan for Brooke Avenue on page 53 has a selectively compressed design to fit in a corner on two 30"-long bookcases. This is the fifth layout design I have published for this area, and it is the most compact. It captures much of the operation of the yard despite its small size.

New York, Philadelphia & Norfolk Railroad started in 1882 as a way to link the Northeast—and Virginia's eastern shore—with the Norfolk area and bypass the congested Washington, D.C., route. In 1885, it started operating a car float over a 36-mile route from Cape Charles to Norfolk at the mouth of the western branch of the Elizabeth River. The Pennsylvania Railroad leased the NYP&N in 1920 and effectively took over. In 1929, the PRR acquired trackage rights over the Norfolk Southern (not the same railroad as the current NS), allowing it to relocate the car float terminal to Little Creek, Virginia, and reduce the car float distance to 26 miles. The car float remained in sporadic service until 2013 as part of the Bay Coast Railroad, a short line spun off from the current NS (the latest owner of the NYP&N after PRR and Penn Central). It is now permanently idled.

New York City Harbor

While car floats operated across the continent, it was in New York City Harbor where railroad marine operations grew to unmatched size and scope, **10**. The geography of the harbor and the history of its industrial development contributed to this. Four of the five boroughs of New York City are on islands. Even before railroads developed, the city had extensive industrial development along the shores of its fine natural harbor, something hard to appreciate today as it is largely gone.

Manhattan had only one railroad serving it via an all-land route, Vanderbilt's New York Central. Prior to 1917, there were no rail links to Brooklyn, Queens, or Long Island that were usable by freight trains. To reach those boroughs with their extensive waterfront industries, railroads from the south and west had to travel up the west side of the Hudson River via the West Shore Railroad as far north as Albany. Then they crossed the Hudson River and turned south, following New York Central tracks to Manhattan. Freight traffic going to Brooklyn, Queens, Staten Island, or Long Island then had to be unloaded and either carted or put on lighters to the final destination.

In 1917, completion of the Hell Gate Bridge between the Bronx and Queens improved the situation, but the all-rail route was still torturous. In 1924, construction of the Castleton Bridge south of Albany reduced the overall travel distance of the west-side bypass to New York City by some 20 miles, but a freight car journey to New York City still required two to three days.

The solution to the problem was to ship cargo from the New Jersey side of the harbor via ferries, barges, and lighters to the various locations on the other side of the harbor. This required double handling of the freight from railcar to water vessel and then to another railcar or direct to an industry. It became obvious to the railroads that shipping a loaded freight car was simpler. Using Haupt's experience in the Civil War, the Central Railroad of New Jersey, with cooperation from the PRR, instituted the first car float in New York Harbor in 1866.

The concept took off. John Starin and his company, Starin City River & Harbor Transportation, were especially influential in developing New York's railroad marine operations. By 1880, he had a fleet of 130 tugs, lighters, barges, and car floats. He then sold the whole operation to the Lackawanna Railroad in 1904.

Other harbors on the East Coast had direct rail access to the waterfront. To remain competitive, New York harbor railroads ended up absorbing the cost of the rail-marine operations. Any freight shipped to New York from more than 150 miles away did not receive a charge for marine handling of its freight. In order to keep rail-marine costs under control, railroads began to operate their own tugs and floats. Eventually, most of the major railroads that served New York Harbor had their own car float operations, much to the everlasting delight of model railroaders everywhere. At their peak, New York harbor railroads had 3,400 employees operating 323 car floats and 1,094 other barges, which were towed by 150 tugboats.

Looking toward Manhattan from the Hudson River, Vince Lee captures the look, feel, and operation of Erie Railroad's 28th Street Yard. *Vince Lee*

Vince Lee kitbashed available structure kits and laid ready-to-run track on two hollow-core doors to build his compact layout. *Vince Lee*

Pocket terminals are probably the car float operation that most captures model railroaders' imaginations. These are small railroad yards connected only by a car float to serve local industries. Alice Street and Brook Avenue are two examples around the United States, but there were several in New York Harbor. Some of them had incredibly complex trackwork to fit the site. Tim Warris's HO scale CNJ Bronx Terminal is an excellent example, **11**. Tim modeled the convoluted trackwork on the layout in one-for-one accordance with the prototype. It includes numerous curved diamonds, lap switches, and other oddities like removable rail crossings and a circular freight house. The transfer bridge is a lasercut Howe truss.

Using only commercial track, Vince Lee built an HO scale example of a New York pocket terminal, the Erie's 28th Street Yard on Manhattan, one of several isolated yards on the west side of Manhattan, **12–14**. (See a track plan of this yard on page 53.)

There were two basic types of car floats: interchange and station float. Interchange floats, also called *transfer floats*, could carry up to 22 cars on their flat decks. They transported cars between harbor rail terminals for through shipment. The biggest user of transfer floats in the harbor was the New York, New Haven & Hartford, which floated close to half a million freight cars in 1954. But other railroads were busy too.

14

Colorful railroad tugs are a large part of the charm of a railroad car float terminal. Vince Lee used a Walthers kit to build this Erie tugboat. *Vince Lee*

15

The Cross Harbor Railroad chugs across New York Harbor under the World Trade Center towers in February 2000. Tragically, the towers are now gone, but the car float still operates as part of NYNJ Rail. *Brad McCelland*

Interchange floats are nearly rectangular barges fitted with tracks built to withstand heavy stresses encountered while loading freight cars. Originally, they were made with wood and had a capacity of eight cars on two tracks. Steel replaced wood as the floats became bigger, reaching up to 360 feet long, with a capacity of 22 cars. By about 1900, they were standardized so that any New York Harbor terminal's transfer bridge could handle any railroad's car float.

The standard New York Harbor interchange float had a track arrangement that was peculiar to New York. They had three parallel tracks on deck. The port-side track narrowed

down into two tracks at the forward end of the float with just the turnout frog on the deck of the car float. The rest of the turnout, including the points, resided on transfer bridges.

A transfer bridge was the general name for the type of bridge connecting a car float to the shore. In New York, in 1930, there were 40 transfer bridges in service. There were several types. Wooden truss bridges were some of the first designs adopted by railroads. Later, pontoons, steel pony trusses, and steel girder transfer bridges came into service. Some bridges had elaborate support structures to raise and lower them to match the tides. Included in the support structures were

counterbalances, winches, hawsers, locking toggles, and other features to secure the float to the transfer bridge. Models of these structures add a distinctive element to a layout and help establish the marine theme. Walthers offered a nice HO scale model of a steel transfer bridge and support structure.

Station floats had two tracks that could hold 6–12 cars. They had a central roofed-over platform between the tracks that acted as a miniature pier shed. The railroads loaded station floats with freight cars at their yards and towed them to a warehouse, factory, or ship elsewhere in the harbor. Stevedores rigged gangways between the station float and the shoreside building, and they manhandled the cargo between the two. When servicing a ship, the railroads would park an empty flatcar on the station float. They would use that as a staging place for the ship's booms and cranes to access the cargo that the stevedores manually unloaded from the freight cars. This technique allowed a ship to transfer goods from both port and starboard sides at the same time, thereby improving throughput.

Railroads, steamship lines, and independent operators also used lighters to unload and transfer cargo to flat-deck barges, hopper barges, covered barges, and stick lighters. Covered barges looked like floating warehouses. Stick lighters had small booms to help handle cargo. American Model Builders offers a nice range of lasercut kits of these barges.

Floating grain elevators mounted on barges would transfer grain between barges and ships. Steam engines powered the elevators, but tugboats hauled them around, although some floating grain elevators had small engines and even sails for propulsion. As early as 1871, there were 19 floating grain elevators in New York Harbor. Grain shippers used floating grain elevators until the end of the steam era.

A large part of the fascination of car float operations is the elaborate "dance" that the switch crew has to

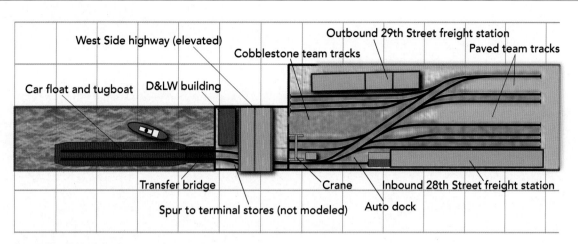

28th Street Yard

Scale: HO
Size: 2.5 x 13.3 feet
Prototype: Erie Railroad

Era: 1950
Style: Shelf
Minimum radius: 12"

Turnouts: No. 4
Train length: 3 cars
Scale of plan: $^{7}/_{16}$" = 1 foot, 12" grid

follow when loading or unloading a barge. Crews had to ensure that the float was evenly balanced at all times during loading, otherwise it could capsize. For New York-style floats, the railroads followed a more or less standard sequence. They did modify the procedure in special instances, such as in the case of an extremely heavy car. It should also be noted that locomotives often rode on the car floats. Some railroads used idler cars to reach cars on the float, but it was not a universal practice.

Tugboats that hauled floats around the harbor are another feature that adds charm to an operation. Railroad tugs, in particular, appeal to model railroaders. In addition to their railroad-specific paint schemes, railroad tugs had design features suited to railroad car float towing. Railroad tugs had a taller bridge so the pilot could see over the railroad cars on the float's deck. Most railroad tugs did not have living quarters for the crews. The crews worked in 12-hour shifts and went home at the end.

Early railroad tugs were paddle-wheel steamers, but the screw tug became popular before the Civil War, and both types could be seen side by side for many years. Steam tugs gradually switched to diesel. Modern harbor tugs use high-powered diesels

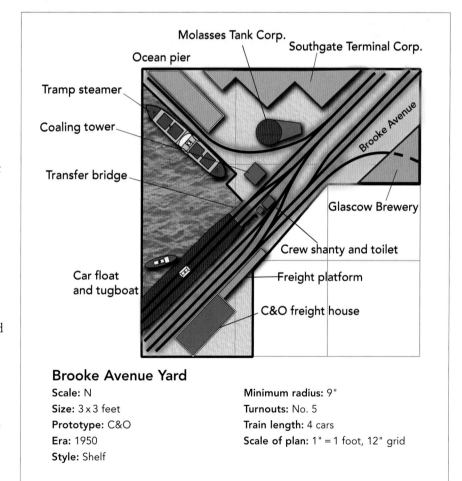

Brooke Avenue Yard

Scale: N
Size: 3 x 3 feet
Prototype: C&O
Era: 1950
Style: Shelf

Minimum radius: 9"
Turnouts: No. 5
Train length: 4 cars
Scale of plan: 1" = 1 foot, 12" grid

and Z-drives, which are ducted propellers that give the tugs incredible maneuverability. However, railroad car floats are rarely used now, another victim of trucking and containerization. Only one car float remains in operation in the United States. It is run by NYNJ Rail in New York Harbor, **15**.

1

CHAPTER SIX

Barge terminals

A large diesel towboat pushes two standard 15-barge tows lashed side by side on the lower Mississippi River. These barges carry the cargo equivalent of five 100-car unit trains or 1,740 tractor trailers. *U.S. Army Corps of Engineers*

Barges are the unsung heroes of the transportation industry. They move about 14 percent of all U.S. intercity freight by volume, while using the least fuel and having the best safety record when compared to trucks or trains, **1**. They excel at moving bulk materials long distances at low cost. There are hundreds of barge terminals in the United States on inland waterways and coasts, and many are served by rail. If a railroad contacts a navigable river, there is a good chance it serves a barge terminal nearby, **2**. A rail to barge terminal makes for an interesting compact model railroad, **3**.

Towboats range in size from about 117 feet long by 30 feet wide to more than 200 feet long and 45 feet wide. (American rivermen call them towboats due to tradition, even though now most actually push the barges.) On United States' rivers, the standard barge is 195 feet long and 35 feet wide, and can be used up to a 9-foot draft. It has a capacity of 1,500 tons. Some newer barges today are 290 feet by 50 feet, double the capacity of earlier barges.

Just like railcars, there are different kinds of cargo barges including flat deck, open hopper, covered hopper, tank, container, and car floats. In addition, there are many specialized work barges including dredges, cranes, pile drivers, and barracks (housing).

Similar to a rail open hopper, open hopper barges carry dry bulk cargo that does not need protection from the weather. Covered hopper barges have watertight covers and commonly carry grain or dry chemicals. Deck barges do not have a cargo hold and are used to move machinery, construction materials, large fabricated items, or a combination of cargoes. Some deck barges have locking fixtures to carry containers. Tank barges carry liquids.

The average river tow has 15 barges, but they can go up to 40 barges, depending on the type of cargo, the river segments being navigated, and the size of the towboat. Because of their meandering nature and varying width, smaller tributaries can support only 4-barge tows. In addition, their locks are smaller.

It is difficult to appreciate the carrying capacity of a barge until you understand how much tonnage a single barge can move. One loaded covered hopper barge carries enough wheat to make almost 2.5 million loaves of bread. A loaded tank barge carries enough gasoline to satisfy the annual demand of about 2,500 people. A 15-barge tow can carry 22,500 tons, the same as 2½ 100-ton unit trains or 870 tractor trailers, **4**.

Barges transport more than 60 percent of U.S. grain exports, about 22 percent of domestic petroleum and petroleum products, and 20 percent of coal used in electricity generation.

2
CSX coal hoppers await unloading at the Winifrede barge loadout on the Kanawha River in West Virginia. The Winifrede loadout has been in service on and off since 1881.

3
My paper mill model depicted a barge loadout for wood chips on the front edge. The large paper mill at West Point, Virginia, on the Mattaponi River served as the prototype inspiration for the model.

Capacities of each individual vehicle

▬▬ 1,500-ton barge	— 100-ton hopper car	- 26-ton semitrailer
52,500 bushels	3,500 bushels	910 bushels
453,000 gallons	30,240 gallons	7,865 gallons

Truck and rail equivalent to a 15-barge tow

15 barges with 1 tug (typical tow)

2½ unit trains with 100 cars each and 4 locomotives

870 semitrailers

Scale of drawing 1:9600

4

Compared to trucks and trains, barges have much greater capacity.

5

The covered barge loading shed at Port of Evansville proudly wore its name on the roof for many years, but the letters are now absent. *Port of Evansville*

6

A steam tug pushes a barge from the Port of Evansville. The barge carries a triple rack of automobiles. The barge and towboat would certainly make an interesting and unusual model for a layout. *Port of Evansville*

Barge shipments are also very fuel efficient. Barges can move 1 ton of cargo 576 miles for the same amount of fuel it takes a railcar to carry the same amount of cargo 413 miles or a truck to haul it 155 miles.

Drawbacks are their slow speed and their dependence on the sometimes fickle nature of the rivers they travel. They are not well suited for shipping the latest iPod or perishable fruit.

Once steam and paddle-wheel driven, towboats now use diesels almost exclusively. The diesel engines produce power from a few hundred horsepower up to 10,000 horsepower. Larger towboats operate on the lower Mississippi where the river is wide. Their flat-bottom design allows them to operate in very shallow water, yet they have tremendous pushing power.

Crew sizes on long-distance towboats range from 9 to 12, depending on the size of the towboat, the distance they travel, and whether they go on the ocean or not.

The crew lives on the boat and works in shifts. They have hours of service rules similar to a railroad crew. Most of the larger towboats include a cook in the crew.

The Port of Evansville

The Port of Evansville on the Ohio River in Evansville, Indiana, has been an important river port since 1856 when it was granted Port of Entry status. The port ships products to various destinations including those overseas.

The port is a good example of a barge terminal on the Ohio River, except that it has an unusual covered shed for loading barges.

Dedicated in 1932, the E. Mead Johnson Terminal covered shed sported a large sign painted on its roof, **5**. Since then, it has had many owners and operators. Northern Ag Service has been the owner since June 2010.

Northern Ag's facility includes about 109,000 square feet of warehousing storage in the terminal building, adjacent to railroad tracks. There is a modern grain storage and barge loadout on the west end of the port.

Over the years, the port has handled a wide mix of products, including gypsum, cigarettes, coal, grain, automobiles, steel coils, aluminum ingots, canned processed food, lumber, fertilizer, electronics, scrap metal, and barrels of whiskey, **6–7**.

The terminal used to ship large quantities of steel coils. But that business ceased when Whirlpool stopped producing refrigerators at its local assembly plant.

The model railroad design is a Layout Design Element that could be built as part of a larger home layout or as a module. The tracks are represented close to their overall length. The warehouses and grain elevators are selectively compressed to reduce the overall width of the layout to ease access.

The covered barge shed is truncated in the layout design, again to save on layout width. However, the portion that is modeled captures the feel for the structure. If you model the truncated end as an open gable, the interesting cranes and slings for automobile loading would be visible, **8**.

The lettering on the roof is not now present, but if you model an earlier era, you can include the lettering.

Built in 1990, the modern grain elevator has a capacity for 1.8 million bushels of grain. Earlier layouts would not include this facility.

The track that runs along the back is a main track for CSX, and L&N before that. At that switch, the main line branches off and heads northwest. It can be omitted if your layout plan does not include that section of track.

Workers load Illinois Central boxcars with sacks of sugar in the Port of Evansville. *Port of Evansville*

The port used special slings and racks to lift vehicles and load them on the barges. These slings and racks would be a fun detail to model. *Port of Evansville*

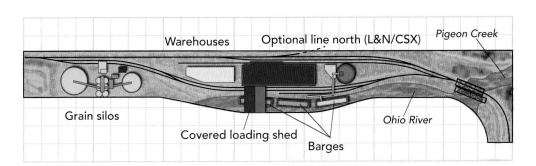

Port of Evansville

Scale: HO
Size: 3 x 28 feet
Prototype: L&N or CSX
Era: 1930s to present

Style: Shelf/LDE
Mainline run: 29 feet
Minimum radius: 30"
Turnouts: No. 6

Train length: 12–15 cars
Scale of plan:
3/16" = 1 foot, 12" grid

1

CHAPTER SEVEN

Container terminals

Two BNSF 6-axle engines pull a short train of double-stacks past Chase Marine Terminal on my HO Port of Los Angeles layout. The locomotives and double-stacks were detailed by Ramon Rhodes.

The surge in container traffic has swept through contemporary railroading, both prototype and model. Heavy trains of double-stack well cars loaded with colorful containers have replaced the familiar boxcars of the past. Vendors offer models of intermodal equipment in most scales. Providing layout destinations for this equipment in the form of intermodal terminals, particularly rail-sea terminals, adds interest, excitement, and realism, **1**. This chapter provides a brief history of containers and describes how to design a model rail-marine container terminal.

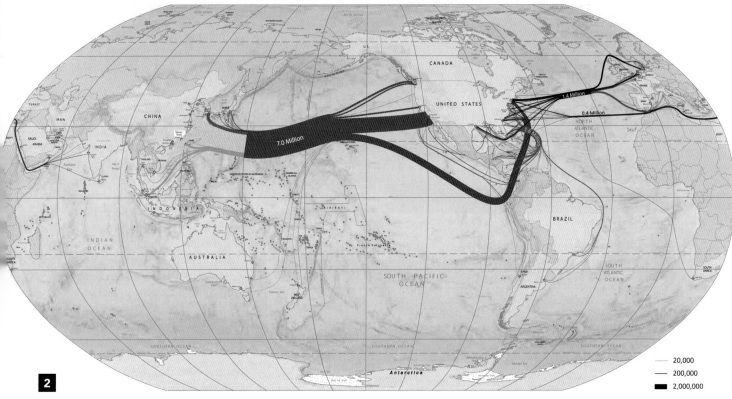

2

Container flows into the United States in 2015 show that approximately 75 U.S. ports received containers from more than 450 foreign ports. Asian countries, especially China, are the major sources of ocean containers shipped to the United States.

Before World War II, a truck driver from North Carolina once had to wait several days at a dock in New York Harbor to get his truckload of cotton unloaded by stevedores. The bored driver was Malcolm McLean, the owner of a small trucking company and natural entrepreneur. In 1956, he bought a steamship company with the idea of transporting entire truck trailers with their cargo still inside. He realized it would be much simpler and quicker to have one container that could be lifted from a vehicle directly onto a ship without first having to unload its contents.

His idea of using some type of shipping container was not completely new. Boxes similar to modern containers had been used for combined rail and horse-drawn transport in England as early as 1792 and in the United States during the early 20th century. The U.S. government successfully used small standard-sized containers, called *conexes*, during World War II. But none of those efforts gained widespread use.

McLean had the vision, necessary capital for investment, a sales force to draw in customers, and the tenacity to overcome regulatory obstacles and

resistance from unions, ports, and competitors to implement the first containerized shipping service.

Ships were a key part of his system. The shipping industry in the 1950s was anything but innovative, governed more by government regulation than competitive forces. McLean's background as a trucker helped him look beyond the ship. He developed a whole new intermodal system of ships, containers, cranes, trucks, and, most importantly, customers. He was also a clever businessman, and he used that business acumen to buy existing shipping lines to bypass certain regulations and also surplus WWII tankers to cheaply outfit his fleet.

He hired clever engineers that converted the ships for carrying containers. In the process, they did the basic engineering to design the containers. Possibly the most important feature they developed was the interlocking connectors that allow the boxes to be stacked securely and unloaded easily.

McLean formed a maritime container shipping venture called Sea-Land. It initially served intercoastal U.S. trade. His first container ship was the

Ideal X, a converted WWII T-2 tanker that could hold 58 containers on the top deck and oil in the holds below. When Sea-Land began service, it had four such ships. This was the first commercially successful container ship service.

In 1957, Sea-Land introduced the next generation of container ships, using another surplus WWII ship, a C-2 class freighter. The first ship, *Gateway City*, could carry 226 containers stacked in its holds and on deck. This became the prototype for the modern container ship we see today, although now the gigantic container ships would dwarf the *Gateway City*.

By 1966, replacing conventional cargo ships with new container ships became the norm. The use of containers in the Vietnam War by the U.S. military opened the floodgates to containerization by clearly demonstrating the utility of containerized cargo.

In the 21st century, approximately 90 percent of worldwide non-bulk ocean cargo is moved in containers. China is the dominant container-trading nation with a quarter of all container transshipment carried out. The United States imports about

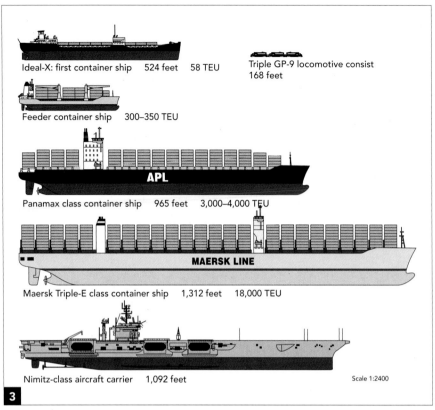

3

From the *Ideal X*, the first container ship, to the Maersk Triple-E, container ships have grown in size and capacity. The Panamax-size container ship is the largest ship that could fit through the old Panama Canal. Ships larger than the Triple-E are now in service.

4

Matson developed the A-frame container crane, built by PACECO, for its Hawaii to West Coast container service. Three cranes were built in 1959 and 1960 for Alameda, Los Angeles, and Honolulu. Cranes on shore allowed shipbuilders to dispense with onboard cranes. Ships without cranes are called *gearless*. *Library of Congress*

12 million ocean containers a year, which is about 10 percent of total global traffic, **2**. A similar number of containers cross the land borders of Canada and Mexico.

Container ships have continued to get larger as shippers seek lower costs through economies of scale. Current container ships are even larger than U.S. Navy nuclear aircraft carriers, **3**. The Maersk Triple-E has a capacity of 18,000 20-foot units and is 1,312 feet long. A 20-foot unit is called a TEU in the industry, although 70 percent of all ocean containers are actually 40 feet long. Container ships even larger than the Triple-E are now in service and on the drawing boards.

A container ship offers important advantages to both the shipper and the steamship operator. Shippers can securely load their freight aboard a trailer at the factory, seal its doors, and send it on its way to the port. There, the cargo remains secure while awaiting a ship that will transport it across the sea. Furthermore, because stevedores hoist the containers on and off ship with efficient gantry cranes, stays in port that were once measured in days and weeks are now reduced to hours. The shipper benefits from reductions in pilferage and damage, and the operator gains more efficient and effective use of ships and maritime personnel.

Many challenges arose along the way. It took a convoluted path, but the trucking and maritime industries eventually came together to develop a set of standards for the design of containers and associated equipment such as gantry cranes. Organized labor had to be convinced that waterfront workers would face a better and more secure future by thinning the ranks to take advantage of the efficiencies of containerization.

Ports around the world had to adapt to handle inbound and outbound containers efficiently, **4**. The covered piers and storage sheds that protected cargo from the weather before hoisting it aboard ship were replaced by large open tracts of land, where teamsters could position trailers that moved on and off the ship via huge gantry cranes.

Some ports faded as new ports prospered. The first dedicated container terminals sprouted up in the New Jersey swamps outside New York City where land, augmented with dredged fill, was available. Meanwhile the wharves along the Brooklyn, New York, waterfront declined. Similarly, in England, London lost importance as a maritime center while Felixstowe became a major container port. The newest generation of container ships are so large that ports have to invest hundreds of millions of dollars for dredging and adding bigger cranes to accommodate the larger ships. It remains to be seen if they prove to be economically justified.

The Alameda Corridor in Los Angeles is perhaps one of the best examples of the changes that containerization has brought about. Construction of the Alameda Corridor was one of the largest public works projects in the nation. The corridor opened in 2002. It cost about $2.4 billion to build the 20-mile-long railroad expressway through Los Angeles. By using the corridor, train traffic moving between the Ports of Los Angeles and Long Beach to the transcontinental rail network based near downtown Los Angeles can move without blocking city traffic, **5**. It included new bridges, grade separations, and a unique 10-mile-long, 35-foot-deep, and 50-foot-wide trench through central Los Angeles. Eastbound and westbound streets cross the trench on bridges.

The global container fleet

There are two types of containers: international and domestic. International containers must meet International Organization for Standardization (ISO) specifications. Shippers can stack ISO-compliant containers on top of one another on ships or on railroad cars, regardless of ownership or country of origin.

Initially, containers did not have standard sizes. Each shipper used the size container that best suited their market. But by 1969, the shipping industry agreed on ISO standards of 20, 40, and 45 feet long for ocean shipping. U.S. domestic containers are 28, 45, 48, and 53 feet to match highway trailers. They cannot be used on standard container ships.

A conductor rides on the last car of a double-stack container train as it backs off the Alameda Corridor onto Terminal Island in the Ports of Los Angeles and Long Beach.

This overhead view of a container terminal in New Orleans shows a typical layout of facilities. From river's edge to the rear are the ship, cranes, storage areas, and railroad-loading tracks. The rails along the bulkhead are no longer used to load containers directly to railcars. *U.S. Army Corps of Engineers*

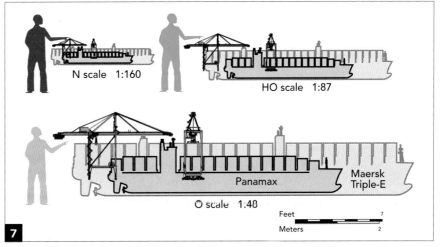

Container ships and cranes have become so large that models in anything but the smallest scales are not practical for a typical model railroad. This figure compares a Panamax container ship and a Maersk Triple-E along with a Paceco 60T container crane in N, HO, and O scales. To gauge model height, the human figure is 6 feet tall.

8

Yard mules, like this truck at Seagirt Terminal in Baltimore, haul containers from the shoreside cranes to other places in the yard.

9

In the early phase of container adoption, on-dock rail was common, as shown in this photo. Cranes would load containers directly from ships to railcars. That is now a rare procedure, as trucks handle the shuttle runs from the dock to the rail yards.
Library of Congress

In 2015, the total number of global ocean containers was about 35 million TEU, while the worldwide container ship capacity was about 17 million TEU. This resulted in a ratio of two containers for every slot on a ship.

There are a variety of different types of containers that make up this fleet. Dry containers (standard and special) comprise the majority, historically about 93 percent of the fleet. The rest are split between insulated refrigerated containers and tanks. Refrigerated containers (also called *reefers*) make up approximately 6 percent of the global fleet. Tanks for transporting various liquids occupy the remaining 1 percent.

Although the size and construction design of containers have been standardized, there can be variations within each size and type category, and by container owner or operator. For example, two 40-foot dry cargo containers can look the same on the outside but might have different cargo-handling capacity on the inside because one container was constructed for handling general cargo loaded onto pallets and the other container constructed to handle garments on hangers.

Refrigerated containers can control their internal temperatures to as low as -60° C, allowing everything from meat, fruit, vegetables, and dairy products to chemicals and pharmaceuticals to travel across the world. Dehumidification systems in reefers ensure optimal humidity. Some reefers also allow the atmosphere in the container to be controlled, so, for example, bananas can be shipped between continents without turning brown. It is because of reefer containers that grocery stores are able to stock and sell all kinds of fresh produce year round.

Reefer containers generally come in 20-foot and 40-foot lengths, with the same general dimensions as that of dry cargo containers of the same size.

Containers on railcars

Railroads haul containers in three types of cars: flatcars, spine cars, and well cars. From its introduction in 1961, the 89-foot flatcar has been the dominant car of the intermodal freight car fleet.

An 89-foot flatcar can carry two standard 40-foot container equivalents. As highway trailers got bigger, 89-foot flatcars became less useful in piggyback trailer service but still could carry containers. They are still used where clearances do not permit taller cars, but the industry has developed more efficient container-carrying cars.

Spine cars are similar to flatcars, but their design omits the deck, which results in weight savings. However, they cannot carry stacked containers.

Sea-Land and the Southern Pacific developed the first double-stack railcars on which containers are stacked two high. ACF Industries built the first standalone double-stack container car (or single-unit 40-foot COFC well car) and delivered it in July 1977. The 5-unit well car, the industry standard, appeared for the first time in 1981. Initially, these double-stack railcars were used in regular train service. But in 1984, American President Lines initiated dedicated double-stack container train service between Los Angeles and Chicago. Transport volumes increased rapidly, and now, dedicated double-stack trains are the norm.

Double-stack cars come in various sizes that correlate to the sizes of the containers they are designed to carry. Well lengths of 40 feet, 48 feet, and 53 feet are most common. Heights depend on the containers they carry. A double-stack car with two high-cube containers can be 20'-2" tall.

Low bridges and narrow tunnels in various locations prevent the operation of double-stack trains. Some Class I railroads in the United States, sometimes in partnership with government agencies, are working to remove obstructions to double-stack trains on their important lines. For example, CSX and government partners are working on the National Gateway to improve rail connections between ports in the mid-Atlantic seaboard and the Midwest by upgrading bridges and tunnels to allow double-stack intermodal containers.

Europe has more restricted loading gauge and train weight limits, so European railroads do not currently operate double-stack cars.

Sea-Land installed this Paceco 40T container crane at its container terminal in Canton, Maryland, in 1967.

I built this N scale crane based on the Paceco 40T crane (shown in photo 10) that was in widespread use around the world.

In 2012, the Seagirt Terminal at the Port of Baltimore took delivery of four Super Post-Panamax cranes in anticipation of expanded traffic of larger ships using the newly enlarged Panama Canal. *U.S. Department of Agriculture*

A CSX engine pulls a boxcar from the rip track on my N scale Seagirt Terminal layout. I scratchbuilt the container crane and container ship (just visible on the right). The container ship in the background is a paper poster, and the container stacks are cardboard cutouts.

Dedicated double-stack trains led to the development of several North American land bridges. Current examples of land bridges exist all over the world, but the North American land bridges are the most efficient, partly because they pass through only one country. They present an alternative to freight shipments across the Panama Canal. For example, containers shipped from Singapore to New York City take an average of 36 days when the containers are taken through the Panama Canal. Using double-stack trains from Southern California to the East Coast, the trip only takes 19 days. On average, transport services between the East Coast of the United States and Pacific-Asia are reduced from 6 to 14 days.

North American land bridges also compete for a share of the traffic between Europe and Asia. A sea voyage from Tokyo to Rotterdam requires 5 to 6 weeks. With a North American land bridge, this time is reduced to about 3 weeks with a typical 6-day railway journey across North America. Yet, this option is not used much, as the route through the Suez Canal using large container ships is more cost effective and reliable for Asia to Europe service.

North American land bridges face challenges as labor and lack of capacity along the West Coast have led maritime shipping companies to rely more on all-water routes to service East Coast ports. The recent expansion of the Panama Canal is also expected to affect North American land bridges by making all-ocean voyages to East Coast ports more cost effective.

Marine container terminals

A specialized container terminal is not necessary for handling containers—but it is faster. Many of the ports in the United States do not have specialized facilities for handling containers; instead, they make do with conventional layouts and handling gear used for non-containerized cargo. In these cases, the ship's gear, dockside mobile cranes, or shore-based fixed booms unload the containers. In some ports, the quays may not be wide enough for maneuvering containers. These require assembly areas near the port where containers can be stored and prepared for loading. However, a more interesting facility to model is the specialized container terminal, **6**. Shippers were quick to adopt these capital intensive facilities because they produce the lowest overall cost. The unique, often colorful, equipment presents exciting modeling opportunities.

The large equipment makes modeling an intermodal facility a challenge. Double-stack well cars with 45-foot containers in 5-car dedicated sets are more than 250 feet long. The cranes and facilities needed to transfer, process, and store containers cover many acres, while the container ships that dock alongside stretch up to 1,300 feet long. Even in N scale, a ship this large would be 8.2 feet long, **7**. In O scale, such a ship is a mind-boggling 27 feet long! To plan a faithful representation, you need to distill the essential elements of the rail-marine

14

This view looks down the yard lead to Seagirt Terminal. Conrail services the Canton grain elevator, while CSX handles chores on Seagirt. The grain elevator silos are only one tube deep on the narrow shelf of the layout.

container terminal into a manageable yet believable size.

Rail-marine terminal functions and features

To model a rail-marine container terminal, you need to consider the major functions involved in the preparation of containers for shipboard loading and then incorporate these in some form on your layout. Functions include inbound receiving, consolidation, container inspection, marshaling, and loading.

The inbound receiving point, located near the terminal gate, logs all incoming cargo. State-of-the-art facilities have automated systems that expedite in-processing. Shippers bring less-than-carload cargo to the container freight station, where agents consolidate it into outgoing containers, while inbound containers move directly to a truck operations yard, a temporary holding area where workers inspect containers and check paperwork. With

completed inspections and paperwork, containers move to the container marshaling yard. Containers in this area are ready for loading aboard ship.

When a ship arrives, yard equipment moves the containers and positions them under the loading cranes. These cranes place the containers on board ship. The ship's crew carefully controls the process to avoid uneven loading that could capsize the ship. They also plan the blocking to expedite unloading at various ports. This is the most time-critical phase in the whole process. The ideal is uninterrupted movement of the loading cranes since this determines the overall loading rate. Whenever possible in the loading sequence, there must be another container waiting ready to be engaged by the crane and hoisted on the ship.

Terminal operators use various systems for container handling, depending on several factors such as the relative availability of land area, labor costs, proximity to other

transportation infrastructure, and local demand. Many container terminals employ multiple handling systems to tailor their operation to local conditions. So there is ample justification for including several different container-handling systems in a model terminal.

The first system used was simply keeping containers on trailers and then pulling them by yard tractors, **8**. This system requires the largest area but a low capital investment, and it affords easy equipment availability. On the other hand, storing and stacking containers on the ground allows better utilization of land area but requires a means to load and move the containers within the terminal. Several systems evolved for these purposes including front loaders, straddle carriers, and gantry cranes.

Front loaders resemble large forklifts with special cradles that can pick up a container. They carry the containers sideways, so they require wide aisles, but they can double or triple stack, which

The Port of Palm Beach uses a rebuilt GP-38 painted in an attractive aqua-colored scheme to handle switching duties.

Gottwald mobile harbor cranes unload containers at the Port of Palm Beach. HO scale die-cast models of these cranes are available. On the left is a Kalmar straddle carrier.

permits higher utilization of land. They can unload containers from railcars or from inbound trailers. In a prototype, operator visibility can be a problem since the container is carried in an elevated position, but this is not a concern in our models. Walthers stocks HO models of this vehicle, while an N scale model was once produced by N Scale of Nevada but is currently out of production.

Straddle carriers resemble boat lifts. They straddle the container and then lift and carry it. They can be the principal carriers for the terminal, or they can be used as an adjunct to other equipment. These vehicles are highly flexible in operation and permit high utilization of land area at the expense of higher unit and maintenance costs. For example, experience shows that a front-end loader based system can store 56 40-foot containers per acre, while straddle trucks can double this amount. Thus, for cramped

model applications, straddle trucks are prototypically justified. No kit is available, but you could kitbash a model by reducing the width of the rubber tired Mi-Jack crane kits available in HO and N scales.

A rubber-tired overhead gantry crane combined with trailers for moving longer distances provides an efficient system for terminals that handle larger quantities of containers. Rail-mounted gantry cranes can be even more efficient. The rails provide the capability to support heavy cranes, which can span several stacks of containers, truck lanes, or railroad tracks. Several gantry crane models are available in HO and N scales.

A popular prototype system is a large rail-mounted quayside gantry crane with rail and truck lanes below. This compact arrangement, ideal for model railroads, allows loading of containers from both trucks and railcars directly to the ship. However, direct movement of containers from ship to rail is very rare now as it is much simpler to use trucks or yard mules to shuttle the containers from ship to rail. Ports advertise "on-dock" rail, but they mean that the rails are located nearby on the docks and not somewhere across town.

In 1959, Paceco A-frame container cranes became the first high-speed cranes built for dedicated container service, 9. By 1967, an improved Paceco A-frame was in use around the world, 10. It is an ideal prototype for a container crane model because of its compact size compared to current cranes and its clean elegant design, 11. Quayside container cranes have gotten commensurately larger to support larger container ships. A container crane that can serve 18,000-TEU or larger vessels is a challenging model project in all but the smallest scales.

Seagirt Terminal

The Canton Company near Baltimore started out before the Civil War as a land development company that leased land to railroad customers such as the Northern Central, a PRR predecessor.

At the start of the 20th century, it formed a railroad company to

This view from the Highway 1 overpass shows piggyback and double-stack well cars in the container rail yard on the Port of Palm Beach, one of the most compact container terminals in the United States.

service customers along the northeast waterfront of Baltimore.

In 1967, Sea-Land leased the land adjacent to the PRR Canton grain elevator to create the first Seagirt container terminal.

In 1990, the Maryland Port Authority greatly expanded Seagirt with state-of-the-art cargo-handling equipment and systems including seven Panamax container cranes, which dominated the port's skyline.

Ports America Chesapeake signed a 50-year public/private partnership in 2010 with the Maryland Port Authority to manage and run Seagirt Terminal. Under that agreement, Ports America constructed a 50-foot-deep container berth and funded four additional state-of-the-art Super Post-Panamax cranes, **12**. The new berth and cranes became operational in 2013. The Port of Baltimore is one of only two East Coast ports with both a 50-foot-deep channel

and a 50-foot-deep berth, allowing it to accommodate some of the largest container ships in the world.

The terminal is also equipped with 12 rubber-tired gantry cranes for stacking containers and several container forklifts.

Seagirt is capable of handling 1.5 million TEU containers a year. The yard layout places the storage area directly behind the berths. Immediately adjacent is the Intermodal Container Transfer Facility, which brings the railhead to within 1,000 feet of the bulkhead. The ICTF handles trailer traffic as well as containers.

I built an N scale version of the Seagirt Terminal several years ago (see track plan on page 69). The layout was never fully completed. However, it hosted a few operation sessions before being removed due to a house move.

Thanks to the compactness of N scale, the layout did a good job of replicating

the tracks that support the Seagirt terminal and surrounding industries. Three railroads worked the tracks: CSX, Conrail, and Canton Railroad.

The Seagirt design focused on the ICTF. I simulated the seven Panamax cranes and container ships on the main waterfront bulkhead with paper cutouts on the backdrop. However, the layout included scratchbuilt models of a Sea-Land Paceco 40T crane and a feeder container ship in the basin adjacent to the grain elevator.

To make stacks of containers economically, I printed images of containers on paper, **13**. Then I glued them to appropriately sized styrene boxes.

To allow better access to freight cars, I flipped the grain elevator on its long axis, changing it from the prototype arrangement, **14**. This placed the grain elevator loading shed on the east side in front of the silos. Also, the model loading

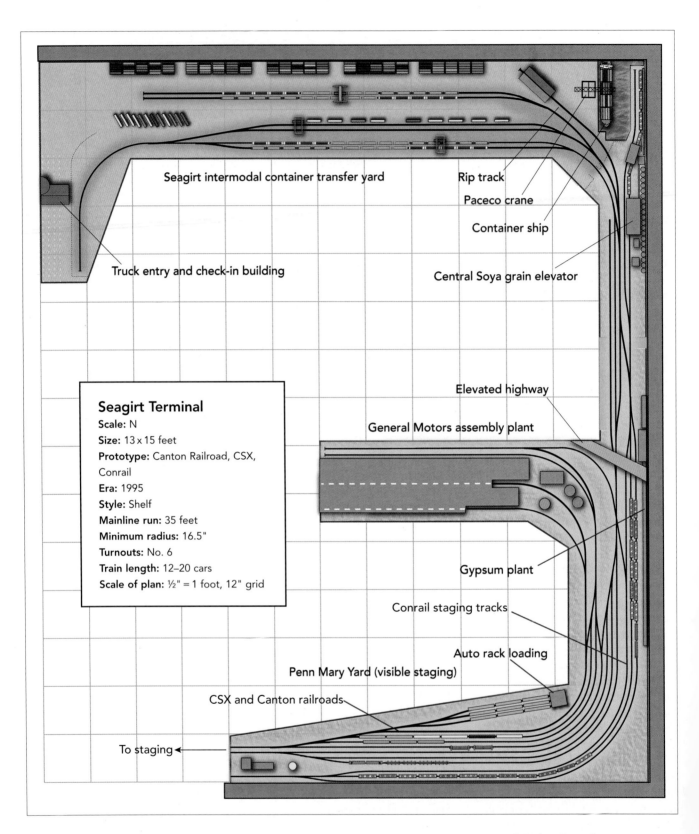

Seagirt intermodal container transfer yard

Rip track

Paceco crane

Container ship

Truck entry and check-in building

Central Soya grain elevator

Seagirt Terminal

Scale: N

Size: 13 x 15 feet

Prototype: Canton Railroad, CSX, Conrail

Era: 1995

Style: Shelf

Mainline run: 35 feet

Minimum radius: 16.5"

Turnouts: No. 6

Train length: 12–20 cars

Scale of plan: ½" = 1 foot, 12" grid

Elevated highway

General Motors assembly plant

Gypsum plant

Conrail staging tracks

Auto rack loading

Penn Mary Yard (visible staging)

CSX and Canton railroads

To staging ◄

shed had two loading tracks instead of prototype's three. Conrail engines switched the grain elevator from their own tracks behind Penn Mary Yard. Conrail also had a diamond crossing over CSX to allow access to yard tracks for the General Motors assembly plant.

As represented on the layout, many prototype facilities, such as the General Motors plant and the grain elevator, are now gone or no longer get rail service. However, Seagirt and the ICTF are still very busy.

Port of Palm Beach

Modelers of scales larger than N face a challenge in building container terminals in reasonable spaces. However, across the United States, there are several busy, reasonably sized ports that are good subjects for model railroads.

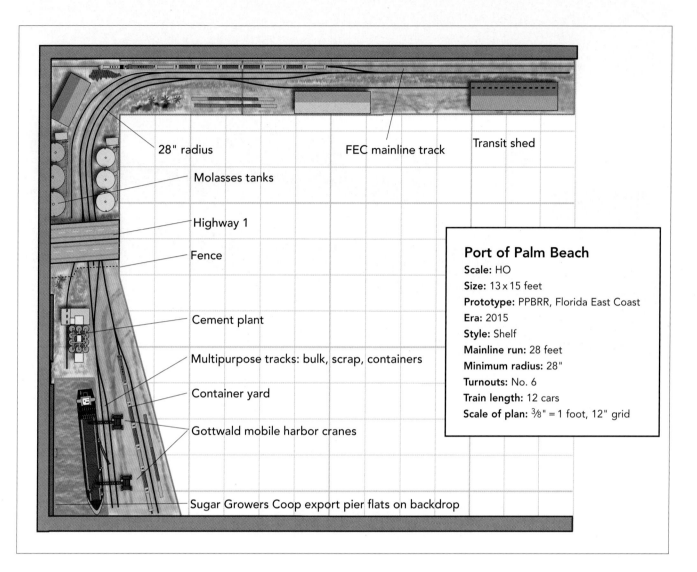

28" radius

FEC mainline track

Transit shed

Molasses tanks

Highway 1

Fence

Cement plant

Multipurpose tracks: bulk, scrap, containers

Container yard

Gottwald mobile harbor cranes

Sugar Growers Coop export pier flats on backdrop

Port of Palm Beach
Scale: HO
Size: 13 x 15 feet
Prototype: PPBRR, Florida East Coast
Era: 2015
Style: Shelf
Mainline run: 28 feet
Minimum radius: 28"
Turnouts: No. 6
Train length: 12 cars
Scale of plan: ⅜" = 1 foot, 12" grid

The Port of Palm Beach in West Palm Beach, Florida, is a great example of a marine container terminal that can be modeled in nearly full scale in 13 x 15 feet in HO.

The compact Port of Palm Beach is one of the 20 busiest container ports in the United States. It handles about 2 million tons a year of a full range of cargoes including containers, dry bulk, liquid bulk, break bulk, roll-on/roll-off (Ro-Ro), and heavy-lift cargoes. It also handles cruise ships with more than 310,000 passengers a year.

Unlike most U.S. ports, it is primarily an export port, with approximately 80 percent of its cargo shipped all over the world. The port supplies 60 percent of everything consumed in the Bahamas, and it is an essential lifeline to the rest of the Caribbean.

At one time, the West Indies Fruit and Steamship Company ran a railroad car ferry to Havana, Cuba, which was the primary rail operation at the port (see chapter 5). It ceased in 1961, when relations between the two nations deteriorated.

Now, in an average year, the port switches about 2,500 railcars. The Florida East Coast brings the cars to the port and drops them on the interchange track. The port uses a single engine to get the cars and handle the required switching. It recently replaced an older SW-1 painted in a red, white, and blue scheme with an aqua-colored, rebuilt GP-38-2, **15**.

The layout design depicts nearly all the port's railroad activities with very little selective compression on a shelf layout that is 13 by 15 feet. The plan includes a single track from the FEC main line, which also acts as a visible staging track. The FEC trains would use the crossover to pull outbound cars and drop off inbound cars on the interchange track.

There, the PPBRR switcher picks up the cars and brings them into the port. Intermodal cars, tank cars with asphalt and molasses, boxcars, gondolas with scrap, and covered hoppers with sugar or cement are typical cars (and cargoes) switched at the port. The port also gets project and heavy-lift cargo, some which is shipped out by rail on heavy-duty cars.

The port relies on Gottwald mobile harbor cranes for many heavy-lifting tasks, although other mobile cranes are available, **16**. Reach stackers and straddle carriers take care of the on-terminal container lifting and shuttling chores.

The Sugar Growers structure is the largest on the layout. This design depicts it as a flat along the backdrop.

Highway 1 makes a great spot from which to view the port, and it is included on the plan, **17**.

CHAPTER EIGHT

Project layout: Port of Los Angeles

Three BNSF engines pull a loaded train out of the Pasha Stevedoring Terminal. Ramon Rhodes owns and detailed the locomotives. The distinctive stucco pier shed (as seen prototypically on the opposite page) is a signature structure on the model railroad.

With a volume of more than 7.5 million containers a year, the twin ports of Los Angeles and Long Beach are the busiest container ports in the United States. But the area is more than just a series of container terminals. In its 16 square miles, there are dozens of other terminals and wharves for break bulk, project cargo, liquid bulk, scrap metal, bulk mineral, and aggregate terminals. There are also fishing boat docks, ferry boat ramps, and cruise ship terminals. When those operations are included, the twin ports are the third busiest in the world.

I took this prototype image of a BNSF consist switching steel slab cars at the Pasha Stevedoring Terminal on a gorgeous spring afternoon in 2014. Replicating this scene was a primary objective of the project layout.

While containers are the main business of the ships and railroads in the port, this project layout features Mormon Island, a small section of the Port of Los Angeles that does not get a lot of container traffic.

Mormon Island was originally a sandbar in San Pedro Bay. After a century and a half of dredging, filling, and construction, it is now a peninsula surrounded by basins and man-made islands of the Port of Los Angeles. Mormon Island is largely an industrial area with no homes and few retail business. The industries on the island have changed over the years. In the contemporary time period that this layout models, the primary industries are the Rio Tinto Borax factory, Pasha Stevedoring Terminal, and three petroleum terminals. Only Rio Tinto and Pasha are served by rail now, and the Pacific Harbor Line (PHL) serves these industries.

Pacific Harbor Line

In the steam and transition eras, "Assigned to the Harbor Belt" was a phrase often heard among trainmen, clerks, and other railroad employees around Los Angeles Harbor. Formed on June 1, 1929, after five years of negotiations, the Harbor Belt Line was a joint operating agency set up by agreement between the City of Los Angeles and four railroads—Pacific Electric, Southern Pacific, Union Pacific, and Santa Fe—to conduct unified switching service at the harbor. Each participant in the agreement furnished its quota of employees and equipment to run the railroad over 117 miles of track.

While this arrangement worked for many years, the rise in containerization in the 1970s and 1980s greatly expanded business in the port. Some shippers had problems getting their goods to or from the port because the

tracks were owned by the different Class 1 railroads that supported the Harbor Belt Line. To level the playing field, the port authorities took ownership of most of the harbor tracks in 1988. They then leased the tracks to the newly formed Pacific Harbor Line, a private company owned by the Anacostia & Pacific Company, which would act as neutral party. The PHL became responsible for making up and breaking up trains, storing and classifying cars, and serving the industries within the harbor.

Today, PHL provides all rail movements on 75 miles of port-owned track. It offers interline, intra plant, intra-terminal, and inter-terminal switching; car storage; unit train movement; and intermodal car repositioning. It dispatches all BNSF and UP trains within the ports, and serves nine on-dock intermodal terminals.

The white buildings in the foreground of this aerial view of Mormon Island comprise the borax factory, while Pasha Stevedoring is in the right background. The oil terminals take up a lot of area, but they are not rail served. *Port of Los Angeles*

Crews from Pasha Stevedoring stack new 53-foot domestic containers as they come off Gearbulk's general cargo ship *Finch Arrow*. The containers are too long for standard container ships and must be carried as project cargo in the ship.

Westbound intermodal container trains that arrive at the port hand their trains off to PHL, and PHL can use those locomotives, or it can swap them with PHL locomotives. PHL crews take the trains to various marine terminals for loading onto ships. The reverse process works for outbound trains from the port, as PHL hands off those trains to UP or BNSF at their respective yards.

Container traffic is the majority of the work with more than 2.4 million containers moved on the PHL in a year, which is about one-third of all containers that move through the twin ports. This works out to about 140 intermodal and unit trains every day.

PHL also handles traditional manifest traffic, such as boxcars, hoppers, tank cars, and automobile racks. That amounts to about 40,000 carloads annually. PHL has additional non-port business switching cars for several industries on the Patata, Reyes, and Carson industrial leads off the Alameda Corridor. These industries include Cargill Milling, PCCR USA, Contractor's Cargo,

International Paper, Epsilon Plastics, Grow More, and Konoike-Pacific cold storage.

In April 2014, PHL relocated from its original home in Pier A Yard to a new facility 2 miles away at Berth 200. The Port of Los Angeles built the new facility to make room for a new container terminal on the old Pier A site.

PHL currently has 25 locomotives. Most are older units rebuilt to modern green standards. The locomotives are being repainted in a black-and-silver zebra livery reminiscent of the old Santa Fe zebra scheme.

Industries on the layout

Four main industries are included on the layout: Rio Tinto U.S. Borax, Pasha Stevedoring & Terminals, Vopak, and Chase Marine Terminal.

Development of borax mines in Death Valley during the late 19th century and early 20th century made California the world's primary producer and exporter of borax. In 1924, Pacific Coast Borax Company opened a plant on Mormon Island. The company is best-known for its iconic trademark—the 20 Mule Team— which 40 years earlier pulled 36-ton wagon loads of borax out of Death Valley. As a commercial product, borax has numerous applications. It is the active ingredient in cleansers and soaps and is an additive in glass, enamels, fertilizers, fire retardants, cosmetics, and medicines.

After several mergers, Rio Tinto, a London-based international mining corporation, purchased the facility in 1968. Unlike other corporate terminals at the port, which are located on public land, the borax plant is situated on private land owned by Rio Tinto. The layout includes most of the tracks, although a bit compressed, that support the borax plant. The borax plant has covered hoppers and boxcars delivered to it by the railroad. The borax wharf is not modeled.

Pasha Stevedoring & Terminals is the third-largest independent West Coast terminal operator, holding several long-term leases with the Port of Los Angeles. On Mormon Island, Pasha operates an omni break bulk and

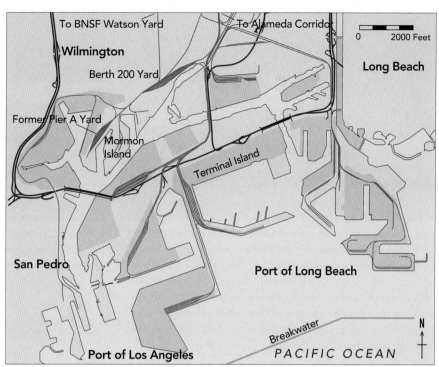

This map of the Ports of Los Angeles and Long Beach shows the area modeled, but not all tracks are shown.

I scratchbuilt the gray tanks from PVC pipe, while the loading platforms and white tanks in the background are from Walthers kits. The tanks help disguise the staging entrance.

container terminal that handles general, project, heavy-lift, and specialized cargoes of all shapes and sizes: yachts, transformers, heat exchangers, 428-ton petroleum cracker excavators, 125-foot-long refinery reactors, agricultural equipment, and windmills.

The prototype Pasha Stevedoring & Terminals facility has four stub-ended

tracks in its yard. Due to space constraints, the layout design only includes two, but they are quite long and each can host nine cars.

Forest products demand careful handling. To avoid damage during vessel discharge, the terminal crews use vacuum lifts to move newsprint, and lumber blades from ships to and from

Lots of interesting and useful detail is evident in this photo of BNSF steel slab cars leaving the Pasha Stevedoring Terminal. On the right are covered hopper cars destined for the borax factory. Behind the covered hoppers is a Mi-Jack crane used for loading steel slabs. In the background behind the gantry cranes is the *Finch Arrow*, one of Gearbulk's general cargo ships. One of the gantry cranes lifts an EMP 53-foot container from the ship's hold.

Steel slabs cut from pieces of plastic make inexpensive details. I painted them with craft paints and then weathered them with chalks. The coils are from a Walthers kit.

On the layout, three BNSF 6-axle engines switch the lead to Pasha Stevedoring & Terminals. The operating gate adds an extra bit of realism to operating sessions. Ramon Rhodes owns and detailed the engines.

At the Pasha Terminal, brand new containers await delivery to domestic users.

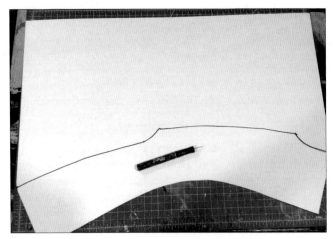

I rubbed chalk on the rails and then transferred it to the Taskboard to make cut lines. I then cut the Taskboard with a new X-Acto knife blade.

I used yellow carpenter glue to secure the Taskboard to the foam surface. I had prepainted the foam with latex paint, but that wasn't necessary.

Masking tape guided me as I painted the road stripes.

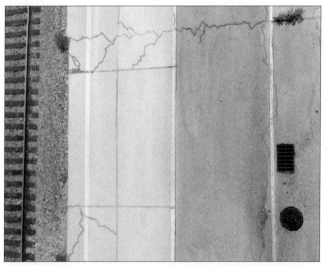

This close-up shows the final road surface after details and weathering.

An Athearn SD-40, now a PHL MP20C-3-1, pulls tank cars from the Vopak siding on the layout. The engine is equipped with a TCS keep-alive sound decoder that allows excellent running, even over the turnouts that do not have powered frogs.

warehouses for storage, sorting, and truck delivery. The terminal currently has a total of five warehouses with about a half million square feet to store weather-sensitive forest products, such as newsprint, liner board, and plywood. These products would be delivered to the terminal in center-beam bulkhead flatcars like those offered by ExactRail.

The Pasha Terminal specializes in handling steel slabs from railcars to ships. Quayside gantry cranes, which are shown on the photo backdrop, lift the 13- to 44-foot-long steel slabs from the holds of ships. Heavy-lift forklifts, with an extra-long wheelbase, transport the slabs to railroad sidings at the terminal.

Then, 100-ton Mi-Jack rubber-tired gantry cranes proceed to load them onto railcars that were jointly designed specifically for this

operation by BNSF, California Steel Industries, and Pasha. These railcars are 52½-foot-long skeleton-type cars that can handle loads of 240,000 pounds. The cars have safety uprights to eliminate slab shifting or rotating during movement. Models of these cars are available as kits though Alkem Scale Models.

As Pasha also handles coils, there are coils and slabs of steel in the

Mike Spoor operates a train during an early test operating session. He holds the switch list in his hand along with a radio DCC throttle. Test operating the layout before adding scenery is a good idea, as you can work out bugs without having to rip out finished work.

With an uncomplicated layout, simple details and a good backdrop go a long way in adding interest to a scene.

I lasercut acrylic to make the portal core. The lasercut parts include the wheel control arms.

I then covered the core with 0.040"-thick styrene. The handrails and stairs are spare parts from a Walthers blast furnace kit.

I test-fit the rotating crane on the base.

This close-up shows the retractable pedestals that I scratchbuilt. I inserted the large upper tubes into corresponding holes in the portal base and then glued them. I did not glue the telescoping posts, so they can be adjusted when the model is on the layout.

storage yard on the layout. They are an inexpensive and fun detail to make.

Pasha also handles new 53-foot containers for use on U.S. highways. Made in China and elsewhere, these containers cannot be carried on standard container ships. Instead, general-cargo ships carry them as project cargo in their holds. The terminal uses gantry cranes and yard goats to haul the containers to storage areas to await further transport by truck or rail. The layout includes stacks of new, unweathered 53-foot containers to simulate this cargo.

Vopak is the current tenant of Berth 187. Berth 187 is on the opposite side of the basin from Mormon Island, but I included it on the layout for extra switching activity as it receives and ships tank cars.

The original plant at this berth was built by Vegetable Oil Products Company in 1923. That plant had the capacity to produce vegetable oil from raw materials imported from the Philippines. It continued to grow over the years, and by 1952, Vegetable Oil Products was one of the largest refiners and importers of dried coconut in the country. The plant produced and stored fatty acids, industrial oils, and refined glycerin. Most of the original buildings have been replaced, and only the storage tanks and an office building remain.

Vopak took over the terminal in 1973, and it operates the tanks and equipment that store and transfer

The finished crane on Chase Marine Terminal unloads windmill blades from the *Danica Marie*. I used my laser to make the wheels and hubs, but Herpa sells spares that would work as well. The ship is kitbashed from a Deans Marine kit. The windmill blades are resin parts from Highball Decals. I scratchbuilt the windmill support cradles with lasercut acrylic.

liquid oil products, chemicals, vegetable oils, and liquefied gases between ships, trucks, and rail.

Chase Marine Terminal is a freelanced terminal that I included on the layout for extra switching opportunities. (This has become somewhat of a family tradition, as it is the third time I have built a model marine terminal that is named after my son Chase.) The terminal features two on-dock tracks where cargo can be

loaded directly from rail to ship. This arrangement of tracks on wharves is becoming less common now, but it is still used in many places in the United States.

The terminal has a Gottwald mobile harbor crane mounted on a scratchbuilt rubber-tired portal base. Portal bases allow trucks and trains to pass under the crane. Terminals use the portal bases in confined and narrow wharves where space is at a

A venerable Santa Fe Dash-8 works the sidings deep in Pasha Stevedoring while the gate guard looks on. The gates and check-in building are Alkem Scale Models kits.

premium. Such was the case in Chase Marine Terminal, where the storage yard adjacent to the wharf is quite narrow.

The crane started as a die-cast model from Mannesmann Dematic AG in Germany, which I got from a U.S. vendor. I removed the rubber-tired base from the kit and scratchbuilt the portal from acrylic, styrene, and parts from a Walthers blast furnace kit. I used prototype photos of actual portal bases to guide me, but my model is not based on a single prototype. I used acrylic as a core since I wanted the base to be strong enough to support the die-cast parts, which can be relatively heavy. I also replaced the stairs on the crane portion of the model with spares from the blast furnace kit. The stairs that came with the die-cast kit were very crude. With the model assembled, I weathered it slightly and added a sign to the sides of the crane.

Layout construction

I constructed the layout frames with 1 x 3 lumber and foam sheets. The frames sit on Ikea Ivar shelves, which made construction simple. Since the layout is in my crew lounge and TV viewing area, I stained the upright legs a dark navy blue to improve their appearance. I left the shelves unfinished to avoid problems with storing books on them.

The backdrop is an important component of the layout. I normally like to paint my backdrops, but painting the heavily industrial environment of the port would have been a challenge. So I created a 33-foot panorama in Adobe Photoshop using many of the images I took in the port. I sent the file to LARC Products, where it was printed on self-adhesive vinyl. Installing it was easy with the help of my wife.

Modern ports are essentially large parking lots. Modeling the paved terminals and streets was a key task in completing the layout. I used a cardboard product called Taskboard to make the streets. This product can be ordered online in small quantities as needed. It is easy to cut with a sharp knife. Featuring a slight texture, it looks great when painted.

I used latex house paint for the base coat and craft paints for the pavement stripes. To make the stripes, I used masking tape. The trick to minimizing any bleed under the tape's edges is to paint the base color on the taped area first. That seals the edge with the same color as the under surface. Then I used white and yellow paint for the stripes.

Once the stripes were done, I used pencils, artist chalks, and my airbrush to weather the surface. I used prototype photos of the actual streets, which I downloaded from Google and Bing maps, as a guide.

Since the Taskboard is so easy to cut, I added manholes and sewer drains. The sewer drains along the foreground reward the curious viewer with a look into actual holes that make them appear very realistic.

Fences are another important element of a modern port. Since the September 11 attacks in 2001, ports have greatly increased their security, and now every wharf and rail storage area at the port is behind a chain-link fence.

Fortunately, Alkem Scale Models makes super-detailed HO scale chain-link fences topped with barbed wire, using photoetched stainless steel. They are easy to install and can be used when making operable gates.

Mormon Island does not normally see container trains. In a rare exception, a single Athearn PHL MP20C-3 pulls a short cut of double-stack cars to Pasha. The prototype PHL has a penchant for using single-engine consists to switch the various terminals around the port.

Operations

The layout is complete and operational. To quickly get it in service, I used Micro Engineering turnouts. They have built-in point springs that can be used for manual operation. I did not power the frogs, also to save time. The few engines I use have TCS sound decoders with keep-alive circuits that utilize a capacitor. These capacitors act as a short-term power source, so the layout runs without any stalls or sound dropouts despite the dead frogs.

I have hosted several operating sessions on the layout, and the operators seem to like it. There is enough activity involved so that it takes about 1–2 hours to work through the switch list. The staging yards can support one train, and if we wish to run more than one train, I can also make a new train while operators work the layout.

By virtue of the break bulk nature of the port, a wide variety of cars can be run, making each operating session unique. I made the cargo on the ship deck removable to add variety for different operating sessions, as it can carry windmills, containers, vehicles, wood products, steel slabs, coils, and scrap. It's the team track of the port.

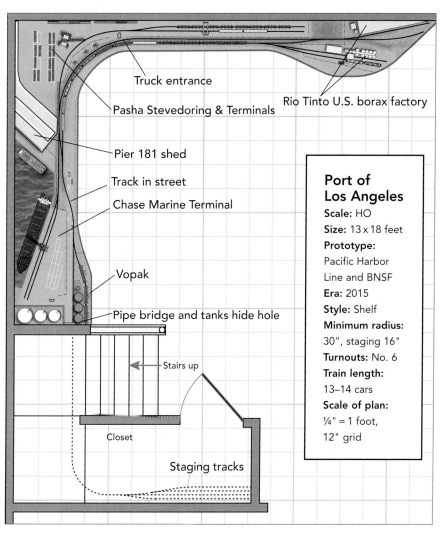

Truck entrance

Pasha Stevedoring & Terminals

Rio Tinto U.S. borax factory

Pier 181 shed

Track in street

Chase Marine Terminal

Vopak

Pipe bridge and tanks hide hole

Stairs up

Closet

Staging tracks

Port of Los Angeles
Scale: HO
Size: 13 x 18 feet
Prototype: Pacific Harbor Line and BNSF
Era: 2015
Style: Shelf
Minimum radius: 30", staging 16"
Turnouts: No. 6
Train length: 13–14 cars
Scale of plan: ¼" = 1 foot, 12" grid

CHAPTER NINE

Project cargo: windmills

A PHL Genset locomotive picks up a flatcar loaded with a wind turbine blade on my HO scale Port of Los Angeles layout. Transporting windmills makes for interesting models and operations on a model railroad.

While the picturesque Dutch windmills of Ruisdael and van Gogh grow increasingly rare, modern electricity-generating wind turbines made with steel and carbon fiber have been sprouting up across the globe. Standing hundreds of feet tall, these high-tech wind turbines connect to the electric grid from wind farms in large numbers, although sometimes you can find an occasional lone turbine as a local power source. Transporting the oversized components that make up a windmill is a specialized form of project cargo that routinely uses multiple modes including ship, truck, and rail.

The first use of a windmill to generate electricity was in Cleveland, Ohio, in 1888. By the 1930s, windmills with capacities as high as 100 kilowatts were in use as a source of electricity, particularly in remote areas where centralized distribution systems had not yet been installed. In the 1990s, new wind turbine technology, combined with high fuel prices and pollution concerns, led to the rapid expansion of generating electricity from wind turbines. Now, a single wind turbine produces, on average, 1.7 megawatts.

U.S. wind turbine installations increased every year from 2005 to 2015, and the United States had the largest wind turbine market in the world in terms of annual wind turbine installations from 2005 to 2008. Wind energy is generated in nearly 40 states, with Texas, Iowa, California, Washington, and Oregon having the most wind energy production. The U.S. Department of Energy estimates that by 2030 20 percent of America's electricity could come from wind power. Reaching that level would require installation of 7,000 turbines.

Most of the current wind energy technology comes from European companies. But some of them are establishing production in their strong overseas markets, including the United States, to reduce transportation costs. Today, more than 400 manufacturing plants across the country build wind turbine components. These components are then transported, often by rail, to their final destination, where they are assembled on site.

In addition to serving domestic needs, these U.S.-based manufacturers are taking advantage of promising export opportunities. The value of U.S. wind-powered equipment exports rose from $3.6 million in 2005 to $488 million in 2014.

Having windmill parts as both import and export cargoes at a marine terminal is convenient for model railroaders. Even more so than coal in open hoppers, flatcars carrying windmill parts are obviously either loaded or empty. By exploiting the import and export of windmills, modelers can justify running cars loaded with windmill

The Port of Duluth, Minnesota, has become an important transshipment point for imported windmills destined for wind farms in Minnesota and the Dakotas via the Great Lakes. General cargo ships carry them on deck and in holds using specialized racks and fixtures. *Duluth Port Authority*

This TTYX car in the Port of Ogdensburg has customized fixtures to support windmill blades, which are visible in the background. *Phillip Blancher*

parts to and from a marine terminal. Alternatively, you can arrange the windmill parts so that they are easily removed from the car to simulate the flow of loads and empties to a port.

Windmill design

Windmills come in various designs. The most common design for large windmills that are connected to the electric grid is the horizontal-axis, three-blade turbine on a freestanding tubular tower. While they can vary considerably in height, blade length, and generating capacity, they all have the same basic design. Their main components are rotors, nacelles, towers, and blades.

The rotor, sometimes called the *hub*, connects the blades to the gear box and power-generation train within the nacelle. The nacelle is the enclosure that contains the electrical and mechanical components of the windmill, including the gear box, brake, speed and direction monitor, and generator.

A tower supports the rotor and nacelle. They raise the rotor high in the air where the blades can be exposed to stronger winds. Usually tubular steel structures, the towers consist of several sections of varying height and can be tapered.

Most wind turbines have three blades. Blades are generally 100 to 165 feet long, with the most common size being around 130 feet long. Modern rotor blades are made of composite materials, making them light but relatively fragile.

The electricity generated by wind turbines must be delivered to the electrical grid. In order to do this,

Union Pacific uses bulkhead flatcars to ship windmill nacelles from Duluth.
Duluth Port Authority

At the Port of Ogdensburg, the NYOG works on a cut of cars with 180-foot blades, the largest windmill blades to be moved by rail at that time (2012). *Kevin Burkholder*

the voltage needs to be increased, or stepped up, for energy transmission. There is usually, at least, one large transformer that is shipped with a wind turbine. This is a perfect excuse to get a heavy-duty Schnabel car on a layout.

Wind energy equipment is not only large, it is very delicate, and planning and handling the loads requires a high level of expertise. Each windmill component has its own special characteristics: the tower is big and heavy, the blades are long and wide, and the nacelle is small and heavy. Because of their height, windmill towers are shipped in sections, while windmill blades travel in one piece.

The multimodal nature of most wind turbine shipments requires shippers, consignees, and transportation partners to be involved in the design, planning, and routing from its earliest stages. For instance, blade engineers try to design parts that minimize transportation costs and still extract the maximum amount of energy from the wind.

Blade designers also develop dedicated shipping cradles for the blades. The cradle designs need to consider all modes of transportation and the securing of cargo for ocean,

barge, rail, truck, and air. Sometimes, the shippers change the fixtures when they transload windmill parts from ship to rail. No two wind turbine shipments are exactly the same, so model builders need to do some research to determine what type they will include.

With these types of loads, there is almost always a truck move at one or both ends, but for the long haul, components generally go by rail and sea.

Ocean movement

When this latest wind energy trend started, an entire wind turbine, including the blades, could fit in a 40-foot ocean container. But the industry quickly evolved, and the next generation of blades became too long to fit into a 40-foot container. The solution was to load the blades and leave the container doors open. Those containers were then loaded on the back of an ocean vessel with the blades extending over the water.

But then windmills got even bigger. The average height is now 260 feet with a weight of approximately 200–300 tons (not including the concrete foundation). They are much too big to fit in a container and require specialized fixtures, railcars,

and trucks to move them. It can take as many as 700 trucks, 140 railcars, and 8 water vessels to deliver all the components necessary to build a small, 150-megawatt wind farm.

General cargo ships typically carry windmill parts. These ships have extra-long cargo holds that have been reinforced for open ocean voyages. A typical ship can carry 10–20 tower sections on the deck plus additional sections in the holds. With each tower section weighing 60 tons or more, these pieces require complex calculations to ensure stowage with proper weight distribution and adequate securing to restrict movement at sea. Loading 20–30 tower sections takes about a day, while lashing and securing takes another day.

Windmill blades present similar challenges, and in spite of their size, their aerodynamic requirements make them quite lightweight and fragile. The units have to be handled with extreme care as strong winds during loading or discharging create difficulties when lifting the oversized blades.

Barge transportation has many of the same concerns as ship movements; however, it avoids many of the road and bridge strength restrictions and varying state-to-state regulations that can complicate planning, permitting, and execution of road shipments. This is utilized either for coastal service or as part of a feeder ship operation.

Railroad movement

Railroads are more efficient than trucks and face fewer regulatory restrictions in moving the unwieldy and oversized wind turbine component shipments to and from ports and between U.S. manufacturing and installation locations. In an ideal world, a railroad would bring turbine components to within a few miles of a wind farm, where trucks would do the last move to the installation site.

But railroads have challenges as well with clearances for the large parts of a wind turbine. Railroad clearances limit maximum width of the loads to 12½ feet. In some cases, trains with wide loads cannot pass each other on adjacent tracks. In addition, a few tunnels in some eastern and western states are too small for the largest components. In response, some manufacturers are locating their North American factories to the Great Plains states to simplify shipping. From there, shipping by rail across the relatively flat terrain is easier than over mountains.

Most of the major railroads offer total solutions for rail transport of wind turbines. They have set up business units that specialize in logistics and planning.

When possible, railroads ship windmills in unit trains since unit trains are generally less expensive to operate. But windmill unit trains have a few challenges. For instance, a train of nacelles might exceed the design rating of some bridges. Railroads can put an empty car, or idler, between each flatcar carrying a nacelle to distribute the load along the track to avoid overloading bridges. For example, a 25-nacelle train would require 25 idler cars.

Railcars for hauling windmills

Since some windmill blades can extend more than 150 feet in length, railroads often use pairs of flatcars, usually general-service, 89-foot former piggyback cars to ship the blades. Shorter flatcars can be utilized as idler cars between flatcars or for carrying a turbine's other components.

TTX Company, the railcar pool service provider, is heavily involved in windmill transport. It provides numerous car types for the transportation of blades, towers, nacelles, and hubs. In addition, since windmill designs vary widely from shipment to shipment, TTX engineers frequently have to design modifications to the cars or adapter fixtures in accordance with individual wind turbine manufacturer's requirements.

Starting in 2008, TTX began converting hundreds of 89-foot flatcars and former intermodal spine cars (each five-unit spine car is at least 260 feet long) to handle windmill parts. These became the TTYX cars that are commonly seen hauling windmills now. TTX converted three different car types to windmill service; single 89-foot flatcars, twin 89-foot

In May 2012, NYOG's SW9 no. 12 sits outside the warehouse building that also houses the Bulk Services offices and the NYOG offices at the Port of Ogdensburg. *Kevin Burkholder*

BBC Chartering's motor vessel *Delaware* uses its onboard cranes to load one of a quintet of used SD9043MACs for export from the Port of Ogdensburg in July 2012. The locomotives are headed to an iron ore railway in Quebec, which has no rail connection to the rest of the North American network. *Kevin Burkholder*

flatcars converted from two TTEX drawbar-connected piggyback cars, and five-car dedicated sets converted from TTAX all-purpose spine cars. One five-car set consisted of 53-foot TTAX cars, but all the others were 48-foot cars. The cars converted from 89-foot flatcars include both raised side-sill and flush deck configuration, standard-level cars.

Additionally, TTX has a large fleet of heavy-duty flatcars, bulkhead flatcars, and 89-foot, 110-ton flatcars all suited to carry heavy nacelles and hubs. Nacelles often require 16-axle heavy-duty cars.

Several model railroad companies produce windmill parts. MicroTrains produced N scale models of windmill parts and railcars. American Model Builders, Herpa, Walthers, and others

make windmill parts, fixtures, and flatcars for HO model railroads. The TTYX cars are not yet available as models, but they are easy to kitbash from existing flatcars and spine cars.

Marine terminals

Keeping up with advances in the wind industry is a challenge that ports, as well as railroads, face. Ports that handle windmill parts must have appropriate on-dock equipment to lift the parts, sufficient land for staging and storage, a trained labor force and logistics team, a railhead or loop track to handle the railcars, and berthing arrangements for barges.

For example, the Port of Vancouver, Washington, has two 140-metric-ton Liebherr mobile harbor cranes (see photo 13 on page 20). When used in

Operations on a layout would be similar to those of a prototype. As seen here, general cargo ships typically carry windmill parts.

tandem, these can lift up to 280 metric tons. Vancouver's heavy-lift capability makes it possible to lift increasingly heavy and large nacelles from the offshore side of a vessel, saving time and eliminating the expense of turning the vessel.

Some general-purpose cargo ships have their own cranes that allow loading and unloading at less developed ports that do not have shoreside cranes.

One surprising issue that ports can encounter is not having enough space to handle large components. Often the port has to stockpile windmill parts prior to construction firms taking delivery. Due to the large size of the parts, considerable storage area may be required.

Numerous ports in the United States and Canada handle windmill parts. For example, the Port of Houston Authority provided the first direct handling of the hubs, blades, nacelles, and towers that make up a wind turbine, loading them directly onto railcars and shipping them as a unit train. Since then, the port has handled hundreds of wind power units moving from Houston to

Sacramento, Iowa, Illinois, and other U.S. destinations.

At another Texas port, the Brownsville & Rio Grande Valley International Railroad, which serves the Port of Brownsville, transshipped 90 wind turbine rotor blades and 30 nacelles, manufactured in China and bound for Iowa. The parts were off-loaded from a Chinese freighter at the port and loaded onto railcars with special fixtures—two flatcars for each blade. The B&RGV interchanged the railcars to Union Pacific for the trip to the Midwest.

The ports of Duluth, Minnesota, Beaumont, Texas, San Diego, California, Savannah, Georgia, and Vancouver, Washington, have significant windmill shipping business. The port of Davisville, described in chapter 2, acts as a staging yard for windmills headed to offshore wind farms, but they generally don't use rail transport.

Canada is also involved in windmill transport. Since 2005, Canadian National Railway has shipped more than 2,100 carloads of wind tower components including tower sections,

blades, nacelles, and hubs. It also participated in the first rail move of twin-pack wind turbine blades. Those blades, which measured 135 feet long, were transported aboard three vessels from the Port of Emden, Germany, through the St. Lawrence Seaway and across the Great Lakes to the Port of Thunder Bay, Ontario. The railroad had to modify the railcars to accept the container locks on the special frames used to nest two blades tip to root. Six trains were needed to complete the move to Dawson Creek, where they were unloaded.

Port of Ogdensburg layout

The Port of Ogdensburg, located along the St. Lawrence Seaway in northern New York, is a compact port that has recently been involved in windmill transport and logistics. It is an ideal prototype for a small model railroad. With its location as the last deepwater port for outward bound shipping from the Great Lakes and served by rail, the Port of Ogdensburg is in a unique position for rail to sea transshipment. In addition to windmills, the port handles a variety of cargo such as electrical generation equipment, transportation equipment, military cargo, zinc concentrate, wollastonite, marble chips, dried distillers grains, road salt, cottonseed, citrus pulp, hominy, and corn gluten.

The New York & Ogdensburg Railway is a shortline railroad owned by the Ogdensburg Bridge and Port Authority. It runs between the Port of Ogdensburg and the CSX junction in Norwood, New York. The railroad is approximately 26 miles in length. The NYOG operates under contract with Vermont Rail System in Burlington, Vermont.

The NYOG is a surviving segment of the former Rutland Railroad's Ogdensburg Branch. Under the Rutland, the port was quite busy transhipping cargo, but its traffic dwindled after 1919, and the branch was almost abandoned in 1962.

The first windmill project at the Port of Ogdensburg was in 2008, when the port unloaded and stored wind turbine parts from Denmark for a wind farm on

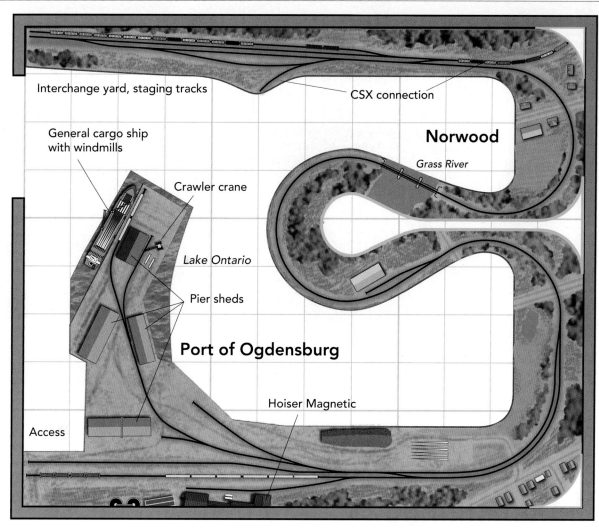

Interchange yard, staging tracks

CSX connection

General cargo ship
with windmills

Crawler crane

Lake Ontario

Pier sheds

Norwood

Grass River

Port of Ogdensburg

Hoiser Magnetic

Access

Port of Ogdensburg

Scale: N
Size: 10 x 12 feet
Prototype: New York & Ogdensburg
Era: 2016

Style: Shelf
Mainline run: 34 feet
Minimum radius: 18"
Turnouts: No. 6

Train length: 10–20 cars
Scale: ½" = 1 foot, 12" grid

Wolfe Island, Ontario. In 2012, the Port of Ogdensburg authority approved a cargo-handling agreement with Transera International Logistics, a Calgary, Canada, shipping firm, to bring wind turbine components by ship through the Port of Ogdensburg for two projects: the Marble River Wind Farm Project in Churubusco, New York, and the Green Mountain Power Project in Lowell, Vermont. That project involved about 10 ships coming into the port, 1,000 trucks leaving, and 210 railcars delivering cargo.

Windmill projects continued through 2016 with a large shipment of Vesta windmills for Churubusco. These blades arrived by rail, while towers, nacelles, gearboxes, and hubs were imported and arrived by vessel.

The layout is a point-to-point design for a 10 by 12-foot room. It includes both ends of the branch. Thanks to the compact size of N scale, the port area is nearly shown full size, while the run between Norwood and Ogdensburg is selectively compressed. If desired, a continuous run could be added to the layout by connecting the northern CSX connection and a track on the pier with a removable section of track.

There are several industries in the port and a few along the branch that get rail service. This plan includes one trackside industry between Ogdensburg and Norwood, but others could be added.

Operations on the layout would be similar to those on the prototype. Prior to a session, an operator would stage cars from CSX on the interchange tracks at Norwood. Then an operator would use the NYOG to bring the cars to the port, switching the lineside industry as it goes. When the work at the port is done, the NYOG operator would bring the outbound cars to Norwood for pickup by CSX. (The actual CSX moves are not modeled.)

CHAPTER TEN

Building ships

A modern ship that dwarfs the trains that serve it can be a focal point of a model railroad. The general cargo ship *Danica Marie* is a heavily kitbashed model (from a Deans Marine kit, a UK manufacturer of model ships designed for radio control). In this scene, it is getting ready to take on U.S. Army vehicles.

Ship models are signature features of a layout with a waterfront railroad. A well-done ship model can be a focal point of the layout. It complements the trains and clearly sets the maritime scene. Shipbuilding is perhaps the oldest model building hobby. Many museums have sections devoted to ship models, they grace restaurants and business as decor, and they can be found on mantle places in homes.

Building a ship model can be a daunting experience for model railroaders. One very accomplished model railroader once said "I'm a model railroader, not a ship modeler" to explain why he did not include a ship model on his extensive port-themed layout. But ships on a model railroad layout are not much different from any other model structure except that they are set on water instead of ground. This chapter covers some simplified ways to make ship models for a layout that are as accurate and detailed as the model trains that run alongside them.

Just like the trains that populate a layout, the type of ships that are appropriate for a layout depends on the era and region being modeled. An early steam layout would have both steam and sailing ships. But sailing ships can be very complex models. The components that comprise their hulls contain complex curves in three dimensions, and they can have extensive rigging for sails and masts.

By the 20th century, commercial sailing ships had become obsolete except for a few cases. Models of steamships are typically not as complex as those of sailing ships, but they still have their share of compound curves, specialized parts, and rigging for cargo-lifting booms and masts.

Ships of the transition era and later have much simpler hull forms than do earlier ships. They utilize a parallel mid-body design that creates a boxy shaped hull with streamlined portions only on the bow and stern. Their superstructures also tend to be boxy shapes, as shipyards build them in sections on shore and lift them as complete pieces onto the hull. These ships can be scratchbuilt employing many of the same techniques used in scratchbuilding model railroad structures.

Several ship kits are available that could be used in a model railroad setting. However, ship modelers normally use fractional scales for ship models that don't exactly match common model railroad scales. Fortunately, the two sets of scales are close (see chart at right). In general, when selecting a ship model kit, it is better to use the next smaller scale compared to your model railroad scale.

A Forney engine spots a car alongside a sailing vessel. Troels Kirk modified the *Puritan*, a commercial kit from Mamoli, for this scene on his On30 Coast Line Railroad. *Troels Kirk*

Howard Lloyd converted this tramp steamer, named *Mileva*, from the *Melanie*, a 1/96 scale Deans Marine kit designed for radio control operation. *Howard Lloyd*

Model railroad scales compared with ship model scales

Model railroad scale	Model railroad proportion	Ship model proportion
O, On3, On2	1:48	1:48 (1/4 inch)
S, Sn3	1:64	1:64 (3/16 inch)
OO	1:76	1:96 (1/8 inch)
HO	1:87	1:96 (1/8 inch)
TT, TTn3	1:120	1:144
N, Nn3	1:160	1:192 (1/16 inch)
Z	1:220	1:250

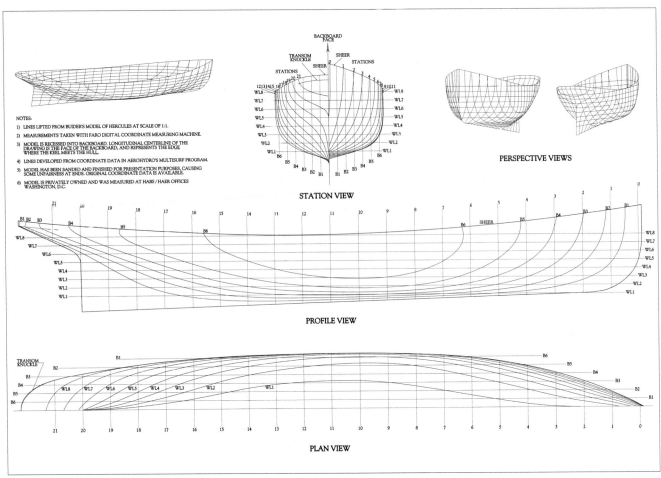

NOTES:

1) LINES LIFTED FROM BUILDER'S MODEL OF HERCULES AT SCALE OF 1:1.

2) MEASUREMENTS TAKEN WITH FARO DIGITAL COORDINATE MEASURING MACHINE.

3) MODEL IS RECESSED INTO BACKBOARD. LONGITUDINAL CENTERLINE OF THE DRAWING IS THE FACE OF THE BACKBOARD, AND REPRESENTS THE EDGE WHERE THE KEEL MEETS THE HULL.

4) LINES DEVELOPED FROM COORDINATE DATA IN AEROHYDRO'S MULTISURF PROGRAM.

5) MODEL HAS BEEN SANDED AND FINISHED FOR PRESENTATION PURPOSES, CAUSING SOME UNFAIRNESS AT ENDS. ORIGINAL COORDINATE DATA IS AVAILABLE.

6) MODEL IS PRIVATELY OWNED AND WAS MEASURED AT HABS / HAER OFFICES WASHINGTON, D.C.

STATION VIEW

PERSPECTIVE VIEWS

PROFILE VIEW

PLAN VIEW

This drawing illustrates the complete set of lines you would need to construct a model of the Western Pacific tug *Hercules* (mentioned on page 49). The lines in the plan view at the bottom would be used to make a bread-and-butter model, while the station view would be used in a plank on bulkhead model. *Library of Congress*

Since this O scale riverboat is under construction on a marine ways, I had to cut each frame in accordance with the prototype plans. The model does not show any planking, but it illustrates the framing technique used in a plank on frame model.

For example, the ship model scale 1/96 (also called 1/8 inch scale because it is ⅛" to the foot) is ideal for a HO model railroad.

Even if you scratchbuild the hull and superstructure for a ship, you still might want to consider using a common ship model scale because you would be able to utilize some of the extensive lines of ready-made detail castings that ship model companies offer including castings for lifeboats, funnels, winches, and anchors.

The most common kit types of ships are solid hull, plank on frame, and plank on bulkhead. There are also styrene and fiberglass hulls from radio-controlled ships that might be usable, such as offerings from Deans Marine and Dumas Models.

Many kits have carved solid wood hulls. These kits are usually manufactured using power carving machines. They can be a bit rough, so sometimes it can take as long to prepare a solid wood carved hull as it would to use a planked hull.

If you are new to shipbuilding, you should be aware that there is a difference between plank on frame and plank on bulkhead models. Plank on frame models have each frame from the prototype accurately modeled. While this creates an impressive model, it is much more difficult and time consuming to build. Frequently, modelers that build plank on frame models leave some of the planking off to make the frames visible. No sense hiding all that work!

Royal Navy Admiralty models are great examples of this type of model building. These were model ships built by ship contractors of the time, probably as gifts to the naval leaders they needed to impress. Few ships from this period survived, but several hundred models did, and these are the best look we have at ship construction in the 17th and 18th centuries.

Regardless of whether you build a kit or scratchbuild, most ships on layouts are waterline models. That is, they depict the model in the water. Thus, the portion of the hull that would be under water is omitted from the model. This simplifies a shipbuilder's task immensely as it removes the need to build the trickiest part of the hull, the streamlined portion that is normally under water.

Converting a full-hull kit to a waterline model can be tricky. The techniques used depends on the kit's construction. If you want to use a full-hull model without modification, it is sometimes possible to insert the hull into a corresponding hole in the layout's water surface. However, on some ship models, partially exposed rudders or propellers can make this a tricky process.

Solid-wood hulls can be cut with a power saw if appropriately supported. My brother converted my 1/48 scale Blue Jacket Company model of the schooner *Smuggler* to waterline by cutting the hull on a band saw. He screwed the hull to a plank, making sure it was square, and ran it through the band saw. Then he used a block plane to flatten and true up the bottom surface as the saw cut was a bit rough.

This solid-wood hull has been cut down to a waterline model.

The simple hull form of this coastal bunker tanker made it a bit easier for Howard Lloyd to scratchbuild. Note that the cabin and intricate detailing are not much different than a land structure. *Howard Lloyd*

The *Isabella* is Mat Thompson's version of an HO scale kit from Aritec, a European manufacturer. The kit is made with highly detailed resin parts and stamped brass details. *Mat Thompson*

I scratchbuilt this short sea N scale container ship for an NTRAK module. I carved a single piece of poplar wood to make the hull. Being a waterline model with a parallel mid-body made the carving task much easier. The superstructure is styrene detailed with commercial ship model castings. The containers are normal N scale containers.

These acrylic parts show the bread-and-butter technique for my modern bulk carrier in N scale. The overall model is about 48" long and had to be built in sections.

I marked the waterline cut on the fiberglass hull with a pencil taped to a Styrofoam block.

Plank on frame models are really not well suited for conversion to waterline models. These kits are usually more expensive than other types because they include a full representation of the actual wood frames used in a ship. It would be a shame to cut away these frames to make a waterline model.

Plank on bulkhead models use fewer transverse bulkheads secured to a longitudinal board (like a super keel) to simulate the hull. The bulkheads are usually solid die-cut or lasercut parts. The hull must be fully planked to hide these non-prototypical parts. From outward appearances, the hull is indistinguishable from a plank on frame hull. But it would be hard to show the interior of a plank on a bulkhead model, say through a hatch or open top, as the non-prototypical bulkheads might be visible.

To convert a plank on bulkhead model to waterline, you have to cut each bulkhead at the waterline. That is easy enough. But then adding the planks is tricky, as some planks will lack support. You will also probably lose most of the keel. So to keep the planks properly spaced, you may have to build a new waterline keel.

For some models, it might actually be easier to scratchbuild a waterline hull from wood, styrene, or even extruded styrene foam, and then use kit parts for the superstructure. This is especially true of riverine steamships, as their hulls have little freeboard and resemble floating planks. Many barges and coastal ships are well suited for this technique.

A few kits from various manufacturers are designed as waterline kits for model railroads. Aritec, Bearco, and Sylvan are three that offer these kinds of kits.

The bread-and-butter technique is a technique for scratchbuilding a hull that is well suited for waterline ship models, especially modern parallel mid-body ships. It is called the bread-and-butter technique because this method uses several planks that are layered like slices of bread to create the solid hull and glued together (the butter). A major advantage of this method—in addition to less cost for material than a solid block—is that since each plank is cut to the breadth of the hull at a certain level, there is less filing and sanding to reach the final shape than with a single block of material, which must be cut to the widest breadth of the hull.

Bread-and-butter is suitable for larger boat models that would be impractical to carve from a solid piece. A bread-and-butter boat model is also dimensionally more stable. Large solid blocks of wood are more sensitive to changes in humidity, which lead to checks and cracks. I have used lasercut acrylic with the bread-and-butter technique with good results.

Several ship kits designed for radio control can be converted to model railroad uses. Deans Marine and Dumas are two companies that offer kits that can be used in model railroad applications. These kits usually have fiberglass hulls.

Fiberglass hulls are easy to cut with a motor tool and a cutoff wheel. I built the *Danica Marie* (seen in the photo on page 86) from a Deans Marine kit. I placed the fiberglass hull on a flat surface and made sure it was sitting flush with the surface. I used a block of Styrofoam to hold a pencil while I traced a line around the hull at an appropriate level. I put a strip of masking tape along the pencil line to make it easier to see.

Then I used my motor tool to cut along the line. It was a dusty job, so I wore my respirator and did the task outdoors. Once the hull was cut, I used a sanding block to smooth the edge of the hull. I then discarded the bottom section. I proceeded to build the rest of the kit in accordance with the instructions, though I used my laser to cut many of the parts instead of a knife.

There are numerous resources for shipbuilders. If you plan to scratchbuild a ship model, you will probably have to do some research to make sure you get the details and features correct.

If you want to include a ship on your layout, but don't wish to build one, professional model builders can handle the task for you. The cost varies, depending on scale and desired level of detail. An HO scale tug boat, for example, would cost about the same as an HO brass steam engine.

I cut the waterline using a motor tool with a cutoff wheel. I used a piece of masking tape to help mark the line. The dust was extensive, so I wore my respirator and glasses.

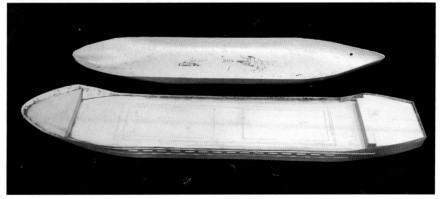

The result of the cut is shown here. I discarded the bottom section. The fiberglass is quite strong but relatively soft and easy to cut.

CHAPTER ELEVEN

Modeling wharves and water

On my Port of Los Angeles layout, a scratchbuilt bunker barge, the *Alicia*, is tied to a dock in the harbor, which features a large expanse of water.

I have tried many techniques when modeling water and wharves on my layouts and dioramas. In this chapter, I explain several techniques that I have found to work well.

To model the large expanse of water, I started with tempered hardboard that I painted with a semigloss dark blue latex paint.

On my HO scale Port of Los Angeles layout, I layered many coats of gloss polyurethane to simulate the water. It is a simple and nearly foolproof method to simulate large areas of water, such as those found in a port. Once you add more than 10 coats of polyurethane, the surface starts to take on a rippled look, just what you want for simulating a sheltered basin. If you make a mistake, you can simply sand it down and try again.

On an N scale grain elevator diorama, I poured two-part resin from Unreal Details to simulate the water in a river. Using two-part resin is a little tricky, as you have to get the mixture's proportions correct, but the Unreal Details product seems very tolerant of slight errors in proportion. Once the resin was cured, I stippled on ripples using thick artist's acrylic gel.

To get a realistic river color, I tinted the resin with a drop or two of Testors enamel paint. A little bit is all that is needed. It must be a lacquer-based paint to work with the resin.

I built the wharves on the workbench so that all the parts were square and level. Then I installed them on the layout as complete units.

Next, I painted on 15 coats of polyurethane gloss finish. After 10 or more coats, the surface takes on a rippled surface, which is desired for a sheltered harbor.

I built a simple wood wharf from precut dowels and strip wood that I stained.

To make wharf pilings, I precut and stained wood dowels.

For the best results, I pre-fabricated the wharf on the workbench, adding the stripwood deck to a framework supported by the pilings.

The finished result has a realistic appearance.

I then tinted two-part resin with a few drops of enamel hobby paint to make the water look more realistic.

After the resin cured, I stippled its surface with artist's acrylic gel to create subtle ripples that simulate moving water in the river.

When I photographed the finished scene outdoors in bright sunlight, it gave the water a realistic depth and sheen.

About the author

BERNARD KEMPINSKI is a freelance writer who has written more than 40 magazine articles and several books on model railroading, many of them on layout planning. He is an active model railroader and has built many models on commission. A former U.S. Army captain, Bernard works as a defense analyst in Washington, D.C.

Acknowledgments

I WOULD LIKE TO ACKNOWLEDGE the following individuals and organizations that contributed assistance or photos to this book.

Individuals

Phillip Blancher, Chris Brimley, Jim Dalberg, Dick Dawson, Paul Dolkos, Dave Frary, Bob Gallegos, Matt Gaudynski, Ghislain Gerrad, Arnt Gerritsen, Paul Graf, Carol Gray, Mike Hart, Clayton Henderson, Dick Knoll, Matt Kosic, Nathan Lafond, Ken Larsen, Vincent Lee, David Lehlbach, Howard Lloyd, Craig Martin, Gerald McGee, Todd McGee, Jeff Otto, Dick Patterson, Randy Rehberg, Ramon Rhodes, Fred L. Shusterich, Monroe Stewart, Doug Tagsold, Mat Thompson, Craig Walker, Tim Warris, Norm Wolf, Kara Yanacheck, and Adele Yorde

Companies

Horizon Hobby (Athearn), Atlas Model Railroad Co., BLMA Models, ExactRail, Fox Valley Models, Hart of the South Models, Tangent Scale Models, and Wm. K. Walthers; Midwest Energy Resources Company and Terex Gottwald

Ports

Duluth Seaway Port Authority, Maryland Port Authority, Port of Beaumont, Port of Los Angeles, Port of Olympia, and Port of Palm Beach

Government agencies

United States Library of Congress, United States National Archives, United States Army Corps of Engineers, United States Department of Agriculture, and United States Department of Transportation

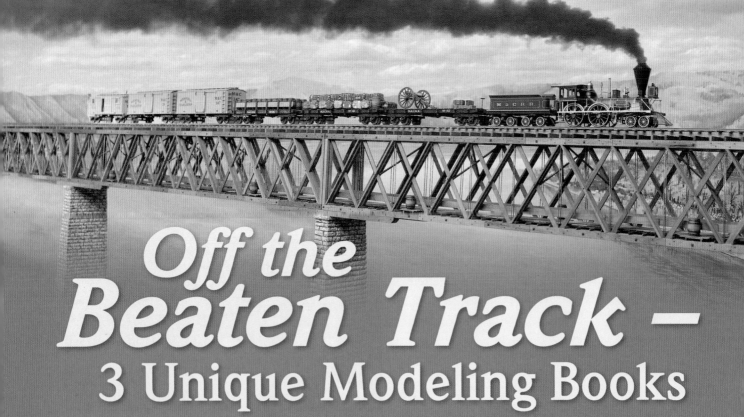
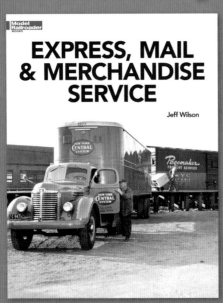
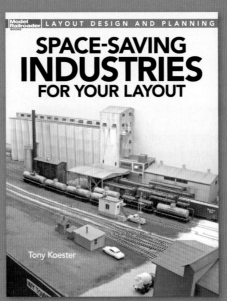
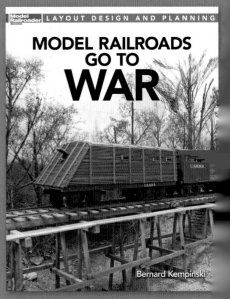